Why Not Me?

My Journey from

Survival to Significance

CLARENCE SUTTON

This book is dedicated to all the individuals who have supported me and my goals; particularly Helon Russell, my stepdad.

CONTENTS

Acknowledgements

My mom, Pamela Russell
Corey Sutton
Austin High School
Student Support Services, Triton College
Coach Gene Metz, Triton College
Jerry Moore, Appalachian State University
Concord Police Department
My Greater Metrolina Mental Health family
My Carolina Therapeutic Services family
Silvia Gardner: 10 years' service with CTS
Ally Street
Justin Woazeah
Steve Wilhelm
Anthony Scott
Silvester Davis
Rodney Clark
Harry Minor
and to Naeem, for connection to this project

1 Austin

My father got me a bicycle.

I grabbed a buddy and said, "Let's go somewhere. Let's see what that Oak Park neighborhood is all about." I had heard people talk about it like it was something special, and I was curious. We lived in Austin, the largest and most violent neighborhood on the West Side of Chicago. We had never seen much of anything else.

It took a long time to ride our bikes over to Oak Park, but the moment we got there, I felt like we had entered an entirely different world. What I saw there changed me deep inside.

How can I describe this sudden awakening? I felt I had been gob smacked. Imagine living your whole life inside a dark, crowded closet. Then you step out and see a fine living room with expensive furniture, drapes, and all the trimmings. Neither of us had ever seen a mansion, and these streets were lined them. It was quiet and peaceful, unlike

Austin where the sirens echoed through the streets at all hours.

Oak Park was for people who had a lot of money.

We knew nothing but the hard streets of the inner city, and suddenly we stood before these iron gates, peered between perfectly manicured green hedges, and saw huge homes that looked like castles from storybooks we had read in grammar school. It was hard to believe real people lived in such places.

The sun seemed to shine more brightly here. The lawns were meticulously decorated with flowers and shade trees. There was no garbage in the streets, no gang presence. These two worlds were as different as black and white, you could say.

We sat back on our bikes and took in the whole scene, wondering about it, imagining what it would be like to live there, until we heard the smooth engine of a car easing up behind us. It was a police car—finally, something from our world. The man looked out the window and said, "Move on, kids. Hit those pedals, go home the way you came, and don't come back."

Even though we traveled the same roads, the ride home seemed to take twice as long, and it was miserable. I felt sick in the pit of my stomach, and I was talking to myself, *Clarence, you can get out of Austin. There's got to be a way to get out to some other place. Some better place.*

I clutched that little thought deep inside me and held on fast, for a long, long time.

Colors

In Austin, we lived life cautiously. You had to think before you so much as walked out on the streets. Take something as simple as what colors you wore to school. You had to be careful about that when you dressed in the morning, because your colors or styles might identify gang connections. If you wore one set of colors, that told people you supported the Four Corner Hustlers. Another color might link you to the Black P Stones, the Vice Lords, or the Latin Kings. They were all around us, each gang had their own culture, and we had to be aware of them all.

I wanted to steer clear of gang life, as I suppose most of us did. But this was another fact of life: you could run, but you couldn't hide. Austin did not offer a lot of career choices for you when you grew up. You played on the streets as a kid, you went to school, at least for a while, and then, at a certain age, you had to find a way to get by. Few options existed and the reality was:

You couldn't get by without money.

You couldn't get money unless you sold drugs.

Selling drugs meant lining up with the gangs.

Many of my friends were pulled into gang life. But from the beginning, and especially after my trip to Oak Park, I was determined to walk my own path. And I hoped that path led well out of the Austin community.

Glory Days

Austin High School was about what you would expect for the

Austin neighborhood – tired, declining, pretty well trashed; a reflection of the streets around it. On the other hand, it got your attention. The school was a looming four stories high and it spanned an entire city block, extending almost to the street. It was "old school" in the literal sense.

Apparently, years before, Austin High had been a different kind of place, a point of pride for the Chicago public school system. On the way to classes I would often walk by a display case which held dusty trophies and pictures of previous championships for swimming and fencing teams— *fencing?* Really? Most of those programs didn't exist at Austin anymore. For the teams we did have, we needed more coaches and better equipment.

Quite a few professional athletes, jazz musicians, and some very successful business entrepreneurs graduated from Austin. My mother went to school there with Robert Townsend, who became a comedian, director, and movie star. Talent came through that place all the time, but those who made it big had to rely on their own moxie. By the time I came through its doors, Austin itself didn't provide many resources or guidance to those seeking a better life.

The school actually held the record for the most attendance at a high school football game. In 1937, the Austin Tigers played the Leo Lions, a Catholic school team, for the city championship. At Soldier Field, which later became home of the Chicago Bears, the Tigers and Lions faced off in front of 120,000 people. An Austin High running back named Bill DeCorrevont, supposedly the most famous high school football player in America before television, was the big attraction that day.

It was hard for me to imagine my high school having such days of glory. I ran my fingers across the dust on those old pictures and thought, "What happened around here? When did things change?" I tried to imagine the streets of this neighborhood filled up with people like the ones I had seen in Oak Park—people with ambition which led to good lives; people going somewhere.

Family

I knew there had to be something else for me. I'm not sure how I knew, but I did. For one thing, I knew about work. My mother worked hard, and my stepdad worked hard. So did my father, Roy, who ran his own business. They all put in lots of hours, and I could see they ran their own lives, took care of us kids, and lived with pride and dignity.

My stepdad was named Helon—pronounced to rhyme with *real on*. He was a supervisor in a factory that did printing, package assembly, and such. He enjoyed showing us the place on weekends—the fork lift, the direction sheets being inserted into the toy boxes, those sorts of things.

Helon was like a gentle lion around the house. Mom was the one who would administer the serious punishment when we acted up. After we were sent to our rooms, we always knew Helon would appeal to her mercy and get the length of the sentence adjusted down. Still, he could be tough when he needed to be.

Mom had gone back to school to get her nursing accreditation, and she was often at the hospital working. Neither mom nor Helon were paid too generously, so it was still hard to make ends meet. At any given time, even with two adults working, we knew the lights might go out because the power bill wasn't paid. "Government cheese" and powdered milk made up a lot of our diet. Sometimes we stood in line at the local church for a food handout, but the little luxuries and extras just weren't a part of daily living.

Mom and Helon were typically at work when I would come home from school, so we kids would play in the streets, in the alleyways, or in whatever backyards could be found in the inner city. Like a lot of kids, we used our imaginations and whatever scrap lay at our feet, hitting bottle caps with sticks in the absence of balls and bats. We would call one backyard Wrigley Field, like the home of the Cubs, because there was ivy climbing up the walls. Another we called Comiskey Park, after the home of the White Sox in those days.

We went outside whenever we could, bundling up with layers of clothing to ward off the icy winds of a Chicago January, just to escape the cockroaches and the rats in the basement, common fixtures in the apartments of that area.

We stuck together, made up new games, and did our best to stay out of the paths of the gangs. A few, like me, were determined to escape Austin itself, the first moment it was possible. Some of my friends figured there was no way out, they just couldn't see their way to get through school and have their lives add up to something. If they happened to have a big brother who was already running with the Vice Lords; maybe that was their chance. Our choices were limited.

One of the problems with school was that most of the teachers were not invested in us. They did not live in our neighborhoods, and they didn't really know who we were or what we were up against. Perhaps the constant battle against street life took its toll on them as well. For instance, I remember watching a teacher really get onto my friend Eddie. She had no clue what was going on in his life, but I did. His father was beating his mother. The night before, his mom and dad were up at three in the morning, screaming and fighting, and Eddie was awake. He was upset about it, and that day Eddie was tired, upset and distracted. But the teacher didn't know any of that, and she was letting him have it.

One day, when I was in fifth grade, we had a substitute teacher. He asked for some of the kids to come to the front of the class and tell everyone what we wanted to do when we grew up. I had some definite thoughts on that subject, but I was also very nervous about standing in front of the class and speaking—I was shy about that kind of thing. Three of us stood in front of the blackboard, and when my turn came, I said, "When I grow up, I'm going to be a policeman, and I'm going to play in the NFL."

The sub looked at me as if I had just insulted his mother. He snarled, "You go sit down right now. You'll never be any of those things!" The whole class began to laugh at me as I shrunk back into my seat. Why had I opened my big mouth? From then on, I figured it would be best to keep my dreams to myself.

Maybe if you show people who you are and get ridiculed for your efforts; maybe if you have enough older people tell you not to get your hopes up; maybe only then will you grow that extra tough hide, like Roy had. Roy was my biological father who was no longer married to my mom. I will tell you more about him, but just for the record, guess what?

I played in the NFL. I also became a policeman. Two for two.

Roy

Roy left our home when I was very young, but he continued to be an important part of my life. He ran an auto repair shop, and spent just about every minute of his time there. He built the shop and kept it going for years, even while businesses around him tried and failed to thrive.

The residuals of crime were all around, broken windows and busted back doors, but the thieves left his place alone. The community also had his back. He was there for them and they were there for him. In a place like the Austin community, that could make a difference. You could make an honest living if you were strong and earned respect.

Roy didn't show me a lot of affection. As he saw it, there weren't enough hours in the day for that kind of thing. What concerned him most was teaching me about hard work, character, and what he called "intuition." For a long time, I wasn't so sure what he meant by that word and what it had to do with life.

When I was old enough, maybe 10 or 11, Roy gave me odd jobs to do around the shop. I would scrape grease off the hard floor, change the oil in a car, or fix a flat tire. But sometimes Roy raised the stakes. He would say, "You have five minutes to change this flat," then he would leave me to it. I had watched him change a tire in a couple of minutes without breaking a sweat. I thought there was no way I could keep up, but he was determined to teach me how to bust my tail and get things done. His belief was, you teach a kid to swim by tossing him into the deep water. One time I got a five-dollar tip from a lady out of sheer sympathy, after she saw how hard Roy made me work.

There were times I would walk home after a hard day at the shop, through tough neighborhoods, and Roy would pass me in his car. I would think, *why doesn't he give me a ride?* He had moved out of our home when he and my mom split up, so naturally we weren't heading for the same home, I got that. But I craved some chance to see his softer side, something other than his attempts to toughen me up.

When I was older, I came to realize that he loved me the best and most honest way he knew how. It wasn't easy for him to make a show of it. I think he knew what life required of him, and he worried that going soft on me wouldn't help me survive. If I didn't walk some tough streets, I wouldn't build my intuition.

A police officer blundered into the shop one morning and caused an uproar. I had enough experience to recognize a drunk when I saw one; and this guy was tanked up. He demanded free repair work on his car. He could probably get by with that, no questions asked, in other stores up and down the street, but Roy didn't hesitate to respond. He pulled out his gun, set it on the counter, and told the policeman what the price would be for the repairs.

Word spread quickly, as it does in Austin, and people showed up just to stand by my dad. Nobody walked over this man—not even the police. Toughness and resilience had gotten him this far, and that's what he wanted for me as well.

Roy ran the shop for thirty years and never had a break-in. One thing that was crystal clear about him was that he knew how to build and run a business, how to gain respect, and how to support his community. When he grew older he gave up that shop. The man who took it over didn't carry the same respect on the streets. The shop was regularly broken into.

Years later, when I was a young man in a hurry to build my own life, my aunt called me and with concern said, "Roy has some kind of deep pain in his gut, and he won't go to a doctor—won't even think about the hospital".

"That's him, stubborn as ever," I said.

"Well, it's serious, and you're the only one who can talk to him."

"I don't know about that—he won't listen to me any more than anyone else."

But it was true; he would listen to me. At the time, though, I was busy and didn't need the distraction. My aunt finally came to get me, with the idea that I could force the old man to go to the hospital.

I was getting my plane ticket, when word came that I was too late. The appendicitis attack had been fatal, Roy had passed away. I never got to say "goodbye." As that sunk in, I felt the sting of self-realization—I was just like Roy. Like father, like son, I'd gotten too busy to worry about what was important.

I know I needed his affection, as any kid would growing up. But he taught me more with his actions than his words. I probably didn't value them much at the time, but I came to appreciate the work ethic he instilled in me; how he handled problems in that matter-of-fact, direct way; and the value of having a good name in the community. I knew he was onto something.

Roy's funeral was a community event. The Chicago Sun-Times even carried a story about it. People waited to pay their last respects in lines that stretched around the block. In Austin, that's about as common as a pink elephant. People live and die, come and go. But on that day, the community came out to honor a man who lived and worked in Austin on his own terms, with respect for himself and for everyone else around him.

I worked with Roy, and I learned from Roy. In time, I came to appreciate him.

Unremarkable

Gang-leaders had divvied up the streets block by block, and we made allowances for them. They sold their drugs on the street corners and demanded payment for "protection" from shop owners. It was not uncommon to see somebody taking a savage beating on the street corner—sometimes there would be five on one.

One day I went to Little Jack Park to see my older brother Corey play in a pickup softball game. At this point, I was too young to play, but I loved watching my big brother. I was wandering around when I looked behind some bushes and found a woman lying there. It was an odd sight, even for this neighborhood. She wasn't moving at all, and it didn't take me long to figure out I was staring at a corpse.

I yelled for my brother, "Hey, Corey! Corey! Hey, Corey!"

He was in the middle of a game, but he could tell by how frantic I was that something was wrong. He came running over, quickly found an adult, and the park was shut down. It was now a crime scene.

That incident had broken up the day's games, but other than that, it wasn't considered a big event.

My family sat down to dinner as usual that night. I sat at the table and told about finding a dead woman in the bushes, then talked about whatever else happened during day. Life went on. There was no expectation or provision for counseling for this kid who had hunkered down next to a lifeless body in the park.

On another occasion, I answered a knock at our door only to discover a white woman, bleeding, naked, and half-crazy. She was apparently the victim of some sort of sexual assault. Helon heard the commotion, came in and threw a blanket over the woman. My mother tried to calm her down and asked some questions while we called the police. I was standing around watching all this, and I can only say it made an impression—but again, it was just another day in Austin, but not a remarkable day.

Even buying groceries was something that you had to think through carefully—what's the best time? Who will go with you? Because it wasn't out of the ordinary to have somebody run up and snatch the bags right out of your hands. If that happened, you just did without that week, because nobody had extra money for groceries.

One day I was walking down Pine Street, going to meet my friend, then we would head onto school. I was wearing my brand new satin Adidas jacket, sent to me straight from Japan. I was so proud of that jacket because Corey, who was in the Marines by this time, had gotten it for me. I wore that jacket everywhere. But suddenly a guy stepped out of the alley and stuck a gun to my head. "Hey, Youngblood," he said, "Give me that jacket."

In no time flat I pulled off that jacket and handed it to him—a gun to the head meant you moved quickly—and that was the last I saw of my jacket. A few weeks later, the same thing happened again and I lost a pair of gloves. I learned what folks meant when they would say, "that's why we can't have nice things."

Nothing I learned in school was as valuable a lesson as having something you treasured ripped away from you on the way there. I lost something I cherished, but I learned what Roy meant by intuition—keeping your eyes open;

knowing where to walk, when to take a side-street, and how to try to be just as invisible as possible.

Indifference

One place I really enjoyed going to was the YMCA, it was one of the few places kids could find a decent pick-up game of basketball. The basket was the right height, non-deflated balls were plentiful, and there was a hardwood floor for the court instead of gravely asphalt. The only problem was that it cost five bucks to get in. I didn't have money to throw around for a game of basketball, but it was possible to sneak in sometimes. I learned which YMCA workers might turn a blind eye and let a couple of kids slip through, knowing they would never actually get the admission fee. One of those YMCA workers, a bald guy, seemed nice, and he would let us through sometimes.

I saw that guy away from the YMCA one day. My buddy Harry and I were playing "Off the Wall," which consisted of bouncing a ball off the wall of his house. Harry's dad was a preacher and peanut seller. There were eleven kids in that house, and it was a fun place to visit. Harry and I looked up from our game when we heard a lot of shouting. The bald guy from the Y was running toward us, with four or five thugs right behind him. No more than twenty-five feet from where we were standing, they threw him to the ground. Then a baseball bat appeared. After they had hit him with it a few times, one of the guys pulled a gun, pointed it at him, and pulled the trigger twice. They looked up at Harry and me, made eye contact for a moment, then one of them walked over to us and said, "Don't be like this guy." Afterward, they all just walked away. They were not in a hurry, they did not run, they casually wandered off.

Harry and I crept over to the guy laying on the ground. He was still alive, but barely hanging on. We could see him struggling to breathe and there was a lot of blood. We were confused, and not sure what to do. We ran inside Harry's house and watched through the window until somebody called the police. Harry's mom grabbed a sheet, walked outside, and covered the body. I remember that she was the only one who did anything for this dying man.

The police didn't come quickly. They came a few hours later, and they were as casual as the men who had done the killing. They did their thing and finally the body of this one kind man was taken away. He would never let us into the YMCA again. We later heard that the incident had something to do with how somebody treated somebody's sister. It was all pretty vague. But that was just another day on the streets of Austin.

While I was attending a college located in the North Carolina mountains, I came home to Austin for a visit, bringing a young lady that I hoped to marry with me. We came into the Austin neighborhood and cruised through the streets where I had grown up. My fiancée pointed out the window and asked, "What's happening there? What's that?"

I looked through her window and saw a lady beating a guy in the middle of the street. Cars slowed down a little as they passed by, people glanced at the ruckus, then sped up after assessing the situation.

"Just a little violence," I said, smiling at her shock. "She's giving him a beating."

"This is not okay," she said.

She was right. Somehow I still understood that.

2 "Fast Black"

When you grow up in Austin, you learn to deal with things as they come up, not too much really surprises you, and you move on. My grandfather used to call me "Fast Black" in those days. A fastback is a car that's streamlined for speed, and my grandfather knew I could always run. I was in a place where it was a pretty good idea to be fast.

I had a friend named Howard when I was in the eighth grade. His dad had gone to prison, and later his mother passed away. Howard was living with his grandparents, and we often played in their basement. I knew this was what poverty looked like, exposed pipes and holes in the wall, that kind of thing.

Howard was a big guy who reminded me of the boxer Mike Tyson—someone you wanted on your side, and not as an enemy. One day I saw Howard, sitting in some guy's car on the street. I noticed something going on with his nose—he was snorting cocaine. I had seen that before, of course, but this was one of my friends.

When I talked to him about his life sometime later and again at different times, he would always say, "Man, don't be like me." Howard wasn't in school at all by that time. Why should he be? He was with one of the gangs, making good money, and his life was set. Some folks I knew admired Howard. Yet he continued to say, "Don't be like me." One of the certainties of my life was that I did not want to be like him.

Still, it was so hard to figure things out. I was going to a school, where the teachers didn't seem to care. In fact, one of them was arrested for molesting a student. In order to save money I walked all the way to school, through the bad places. In Austin, there weren't any yellow school buses that showed up on your street to take you to school. You took the Chicago Transit Authority, and that cost money. So I walked to save my money in order to buy more than the typical "abbreviated lunch," which in itself amounted to almost nothing.

I continued to work at Roy's auto shop and made a little money. But doing so left me no time to spend the money anyway. We worked from seven in the morning until seven at night. My friends would come by and say, "Come on, man, we need you for this game," but I had no other option. If I was going to work, I was going to stay on the job, and there was no middle ground.

Every now and then I would lie in bed at night and think about that alternate world over in Oak Park, with the green lawns and the iron gates, and I wondered what that life was like. Why did they get to live like that, while my only option to ever having anything was the gang life?

The first time I visited Austin High, as a prospective student, it gave me nightmares afterward. I saw terrible things. How was I going to make it there, without my big brother who had moved on? Just getting there safely in the morning was the first goal. There were fights every day, shootings, and young girls getting pregnant. I heard that a drug dealer picked out a nice girl I knew named Ziggy, who was a tenth grader. He set her up in an apartment and soon she had a baby. I remember her friend Amanda pulling a bunch of us together in the cafeteria and saying that Ziggy and the baby were gone. She had tried to break up with the drug dealer, so he shot her and burned the place down, killing Ziggy and her baby.

Howard was no longer at Austin High with me, either. He was well settled into his drug-dealing life now. I wondered about getting through high school, just surviving it physically and staying away from the gangs. It was hard to even think past that—the whole idea of college was up there alongside my Oak Park dream. Not many from Austin went onto college. It took money and the kind of smarts you couldn't develop in a high school like ours, where the teaching and preparation were in disarray. Simply graduating from high school was a big event, and there were many who never made it that far. So if you did graduate, a big party was thrown for you.

What I began to understand was that if I worked hard enough and saved enough money, maybe there would be some way to get out of this place and live another kind of life. Maybe it would be just hanging around in the shop and being as steady as Roy. That's why I had black grease under my fingernails all the time, but at least my nose was clean. The friends who would come by with their girlfriends laughed at me. They were playing more and having fun, but I could also see how they were getting into trouble too, falling into the trap. That was not going to be me.

Gaining Traction

I had one place where I stood out—that was athletics. My best game was football, and as I went through high school I began to show out a little bit. I had always been a pretty good athlete, just playing street ball. But as I got into my teenage years, my skills grew sharper. I was a starter then, and all-conference player. Because of the way things were shaking out, something happened that I had not expected. There were kids in other communities who knew who I was. They would call me by name and tell me what they had heard about me after we played them.

One kid transferred to our school from Lane Tech, which was on an entirely different social level. Lane Tech players had the latest Reebok shoes, polished and freshly painted helmets—and this new guy was telling me, "Hey, Sutton, they know about you over at Lane. They'd love it if you transferred over there."

It was surprising to hear something like that; and it became personal for me, something much bigger than football. Schools like Lane Tech had more than just nicer football equipment. They had parents who came to the games and cheered for their kids. I would often see those parents pulling up to the games in their Mercedes.

At Austin, I was making big plays, winning trophies, and getting named to all-star teams, but there were no parents sitting in the stands for me. We wore our beat-up, hand-me-down equipment and played over at Lane Tech. Yet these rich people suddenly cared about who I was?

Realizing that sent extra adrenaline coursing through me. I would hit them as hard as I could before the whistle blew. I wanted to drag these kids up and down the field in front of their well-dressed parents, so they would notice me, especially since my own parents weren't going to be there. It wasn't about football any longer; it was about life and entitlement.

Fumble and Recovery

My senior year in football at Austin became a milestone for me. I was the quarterback for the All-Chicago team and that was a pretty big deal in the neighborhood. The Austin community took notice. Since the days when Austin had won the championship at Soldier Field, there hadn't been too many notable victories. As I scored a touchdown on the second play of an All-Star game, I felt something powerful rising up inside of me—it was hope, and it was based on something that felt real. I had finally found my escape and could do something with my life.

Between the white lines on the field, the sound of the referee's whistle, and the bands energizing the crowds, for this game, I was as good as anybody in this city. Maybe better. When I strapped on the pads it didn't matter where I lived, or who my parents were, I could make plays. This was football, just a game—I knew that, but it was something. I was seeing a live picture of the dream I was beginning to believe existed.

This meant that now, as my name was becoming known and I was developing a positive reputation, I had even more reason to stay out of trouble. Good things could happen now, but so could bad things, and even faster.

On a couple of occasions, I saw how easily everything could blow up in my face. Of course I had settled into a cockiness that a starting quarterback typically develops. While at school I had noticed a girl I thought was attractive. I decided I might as well make my move, so one day I walked up to her in the hallway and began a conversation. The next thing I knew, all my books were flying out from underneath my arm, onto the ground. Someone who considered this girl as part of his "turf" came up behind me flashing all the usual gang signs and talking trash, escalating the situation quickly.

I took the girl by the arm and tried to walk away. I didn't want trouble, but I also didn't want this guy telling me who I could talk to. I said, "Listen, I don't even want to fight with you, man." He backed down a little, and nothing more came of it for the time being. Later I found out he was new to the school.

Not long afterward, a fire alarm was set off during school. This happened about every other day, and it always meant there was going to be a fight. Someone would pull the alarm, then we would all see who had a target on his back.

The athletes usually exited the building through one particular door as it routed us away from the gang presence. Gang members would then pull up to the curb, usually looking for the subject of their ill-intent.

I came out of the athletes' door and immediately saw the same girl I liked. Now, she was with that same guy—the one who had challenged me. I realized then that he was a member of the Four Corner Hustlers and from the looks of things, they were a couple. Being foolish and cocky, I left the other players and walked over to talk to her. Suddenly a group of guys surrounded me, and that meant blades and guns were also present.

Out of the corner of my eye I saw teachers bailing out and backing away—they weren't going to get involved. They were in survival mode too. There were police present, but they couldn't control crowds of this size; the urban police had learned to pick their battles carefully.

"Look, man, chill out," I said. "I'm just trying to talk to her."

My teammates came running over, shouting and were prepared to do battle. Fortunately some of the gang members respected the football team, and that meant five or six wouldn't gang up on me alone. My nemesis and I would fight it out between ourselves.

Somehow, all the shouting and testosterone ran its course and none of it came to anything worse than a lot of threats. I don't think my rival was really into fighting me without help from his gang. But after that day, he was finished at that school. Whenever, I would pass him in the hall he would just look down at the floor.

I did not see that encounter as a victory for me. As I walked home that day, I knew I had been close to letting my life get out of control. I could have been killed, gotten somebody else killed, maybe even had somebody else's blood on my hands. I could have been locked up, and then I would have had no future at all. Any number of things might have happened, and the one good thing that did, was that I walked away.

It took one more close call for me to finally get the message. My friends Quentin and Tracy and I were climbing onto a bus headed to a baseball game. The coach walked back inside to get some equipment bags. When we would go outside to the street, we always had to leave by a certain door and we were instructed to stay close together. Trouble always seemed to be lurking nearby though and sure enough on this day, a group of thugs walked up to us. We recognized them and knew they would have their guns with them, like always. At that moment, Quentin stepped off the bus, just to talk to them. One of the guys said, "Let me see your bat."

I thought, *No, man, don't do that.* But Quentin, just a nice, easy-going guy, handed him the bat. The thug gripped it in his hands, sizing it up the way you do with a bat, then suddenly swung it into Quentin's face. Quentin went down immediately, knocked out cold; and bleeding.

It's hard to remember what happened next, because chaos erupted. I remember grabbing another baseball bat as the thugs ran away, laughing and shouting. I was out-of-my-mind, furious with rage. I wanted to go after the guy who did it; I wanted to beat him to death. I might have done that, or more likely gotten beaten to death myself. Nothing good could have come from either choice—and when I thought about it later, I realized what a big deal that was. One terrible moment like that, and you either die or get locked up. Whatever the outcome - your future would be over.

Quentin was in the hospital for months because of the injuries to his face and head. His sports ambitions were squashed. Our coach almost lost his job over the incident until our team made a lot of noise about it—this wasn't his fault. But I was changed, too. Now I was resolved: *"This won't happen anymore,"* I told myself. *"I won't ever be found anywhere near a place where something like this can happen."*

Previously, I had been happy-go-lucky about things, living in a raging storm and believing I could walk between the raindrops and stay dry. The lesson that day was called growing up—finding out you are not given a get-out-of-jail free card for going through life. You are not exempt from those life-changing moments.

I had a good home and family. My friends were the best, and the coaches helped me every day. But they couldn't hold my hand through this life. *"There ain't nobody to help me but me"*, was the truth I held onto now. The only way to help me out was to help me *get* out. I had to make an escape from the streets of Austin.

3 Suiting Up to Play the Game

In sports, the term "Cinderella team" refers to a team that has surpassed their winning expectations. The team may continue to be considered the "underdog" as they progress through the season, but they also continue to reach for the ultimate prize. Regardless of the odds, they suit up and they play their best game.

I had a lot of fun playing baseball and football, and running track my senior year at Austin High. But I knew the future was knocking on my door. I did not know exactly what that future looked like, and all I could do was try to stay focused and keep my nose clean.

One way to do that was to play on every team Austin High had to offer. It kept me off the streets. Plus as an athlete, I wasn't going to get locked out of school at the end of the day—I could be at the gym, I could get onto the field, and I could hang out with the coaches and my teammates for as long as I wanted.

Coach Scott and Coach Davis encouraged me to play ball. So I played football, and when football was over I played baseball. And in between that I was on the track and field team. When summer came, or some other block of time that wasn't filled by sports—I worked at the shop.

All that sports involvement put me around men who really did a lot for me. Their job descriptions said they were coaches, but like most coaches, they were also father figures. These men spoke about more than athletics. They spoke about how to be a dad and a husband. They spoke about what mattered in life, what didn't, and how it was possible to live clean and free.

Other males I knew at school were into drugs or some other negative influence, but these men—like my coaches, and Roy and Helon—showed me other possibilities for life. Their influence made a difference in me and helped me realize I could make it.

The door to the future finally opened when I received my high school diploma. Then I thought, *so—what's next?* I still had ideas about catching on with the police department, or maybe I could hang around the shop with Roy and keep on with the family business.

But there was another idea, not a typical one on our side of town—the idea of continuing my education. Going to college might open other possibilities. Not only would I get an education that would make a difference, but I could continue to develop and pursue my athletic talents. But college cost money, and I didn't have nearly enough.

Triton

Triton is a community college on the other side of Austin. John Howard, an admissions counselor, was another man who made a difference for me. As life goes on, you look back and realize how many people did do good things for you when you were younger. Maybe at the time you just took it for granted. But time teaches you to have a deep gratitude for those who made a difference-those who paved the way for you to aspire to a better life. John Howard was one of those people. I have to admit that at the time, the thing I noticed most about him was his impressive afro. I later came to appreciate how he was able to find different ways for me to get financial assistance, and that he even paid for some of my textbooks out of his own pocket.

So, in 1991, I became a student at Triton with plans to study criminal justice. Football was going to be part of that of plan too, of course—I was still in Chicago, and the coaches knew I could play.

My biggest obstacle at that time was the distance from home to Triton. While I would still be living with my parents, I would have to travel about nine miles to school and back every day —and I didn't have a car. If I could be ready to leave at five in the morning, Helon was willing to take me half the way, up to North Avenue, until he had to make his turn toward his own workplace. Then I was on my own. I walked the remaining distance through different suburban neighborhoods, crossed the tracks, through the Oak Park Country Club, out by the nicer houses, and on to Triton. There I would wait for the coach to come and unlock the doors. On those rare mornings when Helon did manage to take me all the way, I was there as early as five fifteen.

Gene Metz was the coach for the Triton Trojans. Many mornings he would get out of his car and see this anxious kid with his book bag, waiting to come in out of the cold—and it was *Chicago*-cold, with chilling winds. The other players would not check in for a couple more hours, so he would say, "Come help me deal with all this equipment," or, "Help me sweep this office," and I would pitch in to give him a hand. He would say, "See those tires hanging up over there? See if you can throw the ball through one of those." And in that way, he began working on some of my ball skills. I had been a quarterback, but he told me my future in football, here and maybe at the next level, would likely be in a safety position on defense. I also might get a chance to play backup quarterback.

What Coach Metz saw in me was a kid who could be counted on to show up early and do whatever was asked. I would not be eligible to play that first year—and there was a certain amount of talk that the football program could be shut down after that—but I was still motivated to be on my best behavior. I was there before anyone else arrived in the morning, and I was there again until evening, because I had no other place to go.

At the time, I didn't realize any of this was a big deal, or that it meant anything. But Coach Metz was taking notice, and he was also passing on what he was seeing to a friend in the coaching profession. He was quietly opening the next door, though I would not find out about that for a long time to come.

Like most young athletes, I thought it was all about what I did on the field. Along with my classes, I was focused on getting to the games and showing how hard I could play. What I was missing was that most of the time, it is more about how you handle yourself *away* from the game. Who you really are is what will make or break you, and that is why a special kid with even marginal talent might get opportunities that a five-star athlete would come to expect.

You also never know who or what will change your destiny. Coach Metz was a good man, and he was one of the men in my life who changed mine. At that time, though, I was thinking about football. What if Triton discontinued the sport before I got my chance? Was this my only opportunity to go someplace where scholarships were offered?

I continued to help Roy at the shop on weekends and between semesters, saving as much money as I could. If school didn't work out, maybe I could go to the police academy. The one thing I knew was that I was going somewhere other than back on the streets.

As it turned out I had only one season at Triton—but my season to shine had finally arrived. I wasn't sure how much field time I was going to get because the defensive coach under Gene Metz, had his own player, someone who had already been there the previous season. Since I was a safety, I fell under his leadership. As a result, I didn't play the first two games. It's hard to describe where my head was at that point. I had spent nearly all my waking hours at this junior college for months now, working out, learning about football. It was hard not to be discouraged and frustrated as I watched the kid who was now playing ahead of me. He was pretty good, but I knew I had something to show these people, I just needed the chance.

The third game was on the road, at a beautiful campus called Illinois Valley Junior College. The game started, and I still didn't get to play. Then I saw something unexpected. Coach Metz went off on the defensive backs' coach. "You'd better put Sutton in, and do it now! This kid has been working his tail off for a year. We talked about this, now do it!" This happened on the sidelines, in front of everybody.

While it sounds like something out of a movie, sometimes life just works out like that. The coach turned and pointed me to the field the next time we went on defense. I trotted onto the field for the first time since high school. On the first play, the other team's quarterback threw a pass, and I picked it off to take it sixty yards in for a touchdown. I came off the field and everybody was grabbing me, hugging me, and celebrating—I will say – I was in shock.

When you wait for something long enough, and it's something as physical as football, you're like a ticking time bomb. I was due to go off, and I did.

The Trojans kicked off next and I was back on the field. The running back came my way and I hit him with everything I had. It was one of those football collisions that makes the crowd gasp. I was functioning on pure adrenaline; it felt like it wasn't even me. After that, I had no problem getting into games.

That season, our team actually turned out to be what may have been the most talented team Triton ever had. We had a defensive end who ended up at Virginia Tech; another guy transferred to Iowa State. And at the junior college level, we had good athletes who played the game well. The problem with junior college ball is that people come and go so quickly. Soon, we would all be gone—along with the coaches and the team itself—the very next season.

Our next two games were against our two toughest opponents. DuPage had a running back named Dwayne Gray, who was averaging 200 yards per game, and several Big Ten schools were recruiting him. He was my assignment. The coach's instructions were, "You're going to mirror him, Sutton. Don't worry about anything else. He's going to get the ball most of the time, so you find out everything about him, how he moves, how he follows blocks, and don't let him go anywhere without you on his back."

This was a new approach to football for me, "spying a single player," as it's called. I went into the film room and watched every play Dwayne Gray made that season. I had never analyzed, or broken down film before, and I discovered how powerful a skill like that can be. If you study enough film, you begin to know what people are going to do before they do it. Because I had no other place to go, I spent countless hours in that dark room, running plays on film. I could see that Gray had a little hitch move, and when that happened, it meant he was about to cut to the left. I paid attention to how he used his feet. He wasn't a big guy at all; he couldn't run over people so he had to make them miss. My job was not to miss.

The DuPage game was played in the snow. My adrenaline came back, and was pumping through me so much that my nose started bleeding. I had to sit out during the first play—all that prep time, and I didn't even start! I had always tried to "keep my nose clean," and now it was literally a problem! The referee explained, "We can't let you go in there while you're bloody, son." I knew the secondary coach was thinking I couldn't handle this job, that Gray was going to run right by me, and then he could put his own player back in. I was on a mission.

I cleaned up my nose, entered the game a few plays in, and locked in on Gray. On the first play, he came around the end on a sweep, I moved past the blocker, and I tackled Gray in the backfield. I felt like I could handle him because I knew how he moved. Then, when his coach sent him on a flair route I was able to force an interception. We shut him down in that game, holding him to less than one hundred yards.

Later, when I was on scholarship at Appalachian State, the coaches told me, "That DuPage game was what caught our eye, in terms of athletics. DuPage in the snow— we saw what you could do against that really quick running back. But still, that wasn't what got you the scholarship. It was what Coach Metz said about you getting there at the crack of dawn for a year, every single morning. About how you worked. Character got you that scholarship, not just football."

I finished the season at Triton strong, never looking back after that DuPage game. My place on the defense was no longer a question. Not only that, but when the season was over, another coach I liked, Coach Holger came to me and said, "Meet me in the gym." I wondered what was up, and when I got there, he said, "Have you ever run hurdles?"

I had run track, but never hurdles. He told me I was a natural and began to work with me. I did what he asked, mostly just to please a coach, but it turned out he was right. I set school records, got invited to the regionals, and ended up flying to Odessa, Texas for the national finals. It was my first time visiting another other part of the country. Even as a newcomer to this sport, I placed seventh nationally.

While I was preparing to graduate from Triton, a two-year school, I was still unsure about moving on to the next level of study. I had played the one season of junior college ball when Triton suddenly announced there would be no more football. The program was gone. I realized that if I was going to keep playing the game, it would have to be somewhere else, maybe some place far away.

Momma Said

I had always wanted to make my escape, but now I wasn't so sure about leaving. I actually applied to go into the military, and also filled out an application with the city's police department. From both places I heard the same thing, "Son, I see you've done college work. If I were you, I'd stay in school. Do what you can to get your degree, and you'll be better off."

At that point, my life could have gone in any of several directions. My mother began to speak up saying she wanted me out of Chicago, because she knew how easily I could fall into the wrong kinds of friendships. Gangbangers were starting to come around, and I was going to go that route "over her dead body". So when college coaches did call to recruit me, she was all over that, encouraging me to sit down and listen.

I actually had offers from a few colleges. All the Illinois schools were interested. Missouri, Washington, and Washington State offered me scholarships. But there was also an offer from a university with a funny name, Appalachian State. What is an "Appalachian?" And what kind of place was Boone, North Carolina?

My mom decided I was going to go to App State, and that was all there was to it. Maybe it was because it was such a different environment from Austin. What really mattered to her was getting me away from Chicago and the temptations there. I did want to get away, and had steered clear of those temptations for most of my life, but I was still immature. At one point I became interested in a local girl, and being close to her seemed more important than my future at that time. It would have been easy for the gangs to get hold of someone like me. But Appalachian State?

I actually did go on a recruiting trip there, but we were snowed in at the hotel, which was off campus. That same hotel is now an App State dorm. At the time I never got to see the campus close-up. But for some reason, without taking a tour or talking to any of the students, I concluded App State had to be a place of prejudice and bigotry, and no way was I going to go there.

But the coaches kept recruiting me, including one who wore a cowboy hat, big ol' boots, and had a mouth full of tobacco. What was a cowboy doing in a Carolina mountain town? It was confusing! He visited our home and stuck those boots up on Mom's coffee table. I wasn't sure he was going to get out of there alive, after seeing the look my mother shot him, but somehow she remained determined to get me to Boone.

Then one morning, I was getting ready for a recruiting visit to Northern Illinois University, in DeKalb, about an hour away. The recruiter came to our place to pick me up, but he arrived at the same time as another visitor, an Austin police officer. The officer was looking into some kind of gang incident, and my name came up, just because I knew the guy. Seeing me questioned about gang activity wasn't the kind of situation that was going to impress a college football recruiter. But the police officer gave me a break. He must have understood that I was in the midst of a huge opportunity, because he smiled as he stepped aside so I could go on the visit. It felt almost like "someone up there" was looking out for me—another blessing.

I didn't attend that particular school, but after the unexpected visit by the police officer, my mom was even more determined to get me out of Austin at the earliest possible moment. Even so, I had another scholarship offer I was considering, but my mother stood her ground. She pulled that letter out of my hands and ripped it into pieces right there in the Triton recruiting office. "You're going to Boone," she said.

Though I lacked a couple of hours needed to graduate, the folks at Triton were also saying, "You're gone. You need to go." And they signed off on my credit hours so I would be qualified to go to Appalachian State.

Within a few days, I was on a Greyhound bus with a little red duffle bag, headed to this place called Boone, North Carolina, to a college campus I had visited once before without ever seeing. As I made my way to campus, I passed crowds of students going the opposite direction. Spring semester was finished, and they were taking off for the summer just as I was arriving.

That turned out to be one of the longest summers of my life.

4 A.S.U.

A long bus ride from Chicago is plenty of time to do some thinking. Maybe even a little worrying. I was riding that Greyhound to a whole new life.

Between Chicago and Boone, we passed through Indianapolis, and it seemed the drive through Kentucky lasted forever. We passed through Louisville, cut across the southwest corner of Virginia, and through my window I began to see the Blue Ridge Mountains towering over the trees. Finally, we arrived at the bus station in Boone.

My new home remained a big question mark. I didn't know anyone else but Coach Moore—even the tobacco-chewing cowboy who came to Chicago and recruited me had moved on. I came with few possessions but plenty of questions.

My first impressions were strong ones. I had only seen this place from a hotel window, under a blanket of snow. Now it was the beginning of summer. Appalachian State has a beautiful campus, located in the center of Boone, surrounded by a constant backdrop of the Blue Ridge

Mountains. There were fifteen thousand students enrolled that year, and even more people wanting to know what was going on at this university.

The Appalachian State University football team, the Mountaineers, were accustomed to winning. They won national championships at the 1-AA (now FCS) level, and then moved up to the Sun Belt Conference. Since that time, they have gone onto play Clemson, Tennessee, Miami, Virginia Tech—and there was that big upset against Michigan in the "Big House" in 2007. The Mountaineers caught the nation's attention that day.

As I stepped onto the campus for the first time, the scenery definitely wrangled my consideration. It was a place of endless beauty, but an empty one. I arrived as everyone else was leaving for summer break. However, I was able to catch up with the football coaches, who were a little surprised to see me. Jerry Moore was the head coach, and George Edwards—now the defensive coordinator for the Minnesota Vikings—was coaching the linebackers.

"You know your scholarship doesn't kick in until September," Coach Moore said.

"I know that, but I wanted to get started early." The truth was, it was more about where I *didn't* want to be.

"But we can't get you situated in a room until then."

"Coach, isn't there some place I can stay? I'll sleep on the floor—I don't care. I just need to be here."

"And you probably don't have the money to get by this summer, right?"

"Yes sir."

The coaches looked at each other, and one of them finally said, "Follow me." They led me to the football stadium, unlocked one of the doors that led beneath the bleachers, and took me to a little room, not much bigger than a closet.

"This is the ref's quarters," I was told. The chains and first down markers were leaning up against the wall, and there were orange cones scattered about. The room was incredibly stuffy with no windows, but there was a shower that the game officials used.

"It ain't much, but it's free," said the coach. "Can you find some food somewhere?"

"Yes, sir. I'll figure that out."

And figure things out I did; at least enough to survive. The first thing I did was to carry the chains and down markers out and dump them in the hallway. I bought a blanket and bunked out on the floor. "I can do this," I told myself. "At least I'm here." I really meant that.

As soon as the coaches were gone, and the sun went down, I kept the promise I had made to myself. I came out of my little closet, jogged to the top of the stadium, found a seat and took in the view. The sun was setting over the mountains, back toward Johnson City in the west. It reminded me of how I felt when I saw the mansions back in Oak Park, the ones I had gazed upon when I was a kid. I cried a little thinking about how far I had come and the journey that lay ahead of me.

No matter what happened, I was here. It was just a matter of trying to figure out what was going to happen next.

I was a long way from the streets of Austin; I had made it out, found a better home, and most important of all, I had a college scholarship to show for it.

Summer of Solitude

Boone is situated 3,333 feet above sea level making it the highest city east of the Mississippi. It gives the Mountaineers an interesting home advantage when visitors quickly find themselves out of breath. I thought that was just locker room talk until I walked across campus the next day and found myself huffing and puffing. I had never been at any kind of high altitude; I'd never been much of anywhere, period, other than the one trip to Odessa.

That first morning, waking up in that closet beneath a stadium, I realized I had nothing to do. I did buy myself a hot plate, found a bicycle somewhere, and rode around campus, then through the town of Boone. I begged a dollar or two from my uncles, and anyone else who might have cared. I would go to the corner store and since I had no refrigerator, I would buy milk in small cartons; I ate a lot of cold cereal. My goal was just to survive that summer, to hang on until football season started. If I had come from some big house in the suburbs, I would have never made it through. But Austin had prepared me for just about anything.

I pretty much just hung out by myself during that first summer session. Weight lifting started during the second session which gave me a chance to prepare my body for the upcoming season. It was during weight lifting that I met a red-haired, crazy guy named Mike Kent. All I knew was that this was the guy in charge of the strength and conditioning program. To this day, he is still a giant in his field, and has directed lots of players to the NFL. He currently heads up the strength and conditioning program for the Florida Gators. But at the time, to me he was just a red-headed, freckle-faced, crazy guy I would see when I was lifting. I didn't know what to think about him, but the weight room was just about the only place I had to go throughout the day. So I would take care of my business and watch his antics. He would walk over to the stereo and announce what music he was putting on, such as "Lynyrd Skynyrd, 1973!" And then he would crank up the volume and announce the next tract, "Aerosmith! 1986!"

The contrast between where I was from and this unknown place amplified my distrust. As the weeks went on, I was getting lonelier and more discouraged. Coach Kent was a peculiar sort, but he was also down-to-earth, and I found myself talking to him a little. I needed to talk to somebody, and he listened.

I still went to the top of the stadium at night. I tried to remind myself how far I had come, but when I cried now, it wasn't from pride but from frustration. I was living in a closet that, along with the summer heat, felt like a sauna. I was sleeping on the floor, and eating cereal or cold hot dogs from the corner store.

Toward the end of the summer, the players started returning. They weren't my teammates, not yet. They didn't know me, and I didn't know them. They were talking about their summers, about going to the beach, and about their girlfriends. When they asked about me, I would tell them I spent the summer in a closet under the stadium. They couldn't believe that was true.

I don't know if you have ever been that age and gone across the country for the first time, not knowing anybody. The whole reason my mom had wanted me here was exactly that – I didn't know anybody. She wanted a fresh start for me in a better place. But she couldn't have known how hard it would be. I was as down as I had ever been, and all I wanted to do was to go home, run back to my past, and forget all this college stuff. That's how I felt when I reached my breaking point.

I was in the weight room when Coach Kent noticed something was bothering me. He kept prodding me, the way football coaches will do, until I snapped back at him and we got into it. I actually wanted to fight him. "I'm out of here!" I said. "I'm done with all this!" I guess I thought the coach would be sympathetic and try to reason with me. But that wasn't the case. He got in my face and challenged me. "Hey, kid, that's all you got? Gonna run home? Just run back to Momma and eat some fried chicken and greens? Sell some drugs?"

His response threw me off balance. He wasn't going to pamper me—he was going to challenge my manhood. Of course I shouted back at him, got in his face, and I was sure we were about to start throwing punches. Then, just like that, I broke down. I started crying.

Coach Kent walked over to the doors, locked them, and pulled up a chair right next to mine. Hours later, we were still talking. I guess because I hadn't really talked much for weeks, the words came pouring out—my frustration, the pressure I felt to make it at this level, and my worries about whether I was good enough. Maybe it really was time for me to go home. Roy would give me my old job back at the shop. There was always the police academy.

"You won't do that," said the coach. "You'd be running away and you know it. You're too much of a man to do that. You don't want to be bitter, looking back on this. Forget the past. It's not where you've been, it's where you're at."

We became good friends that day. He made a big difference then, as he helped me develop my body and mind, not just for this level, but the next level as well—the highest of all, the NFL. Again, it seemed as if God had placed this man across my path at just the right time. It's amazing how that happens.

A Change of Heart

When the fall semester began, I was reminded of how silly I was for thinking everyone here was racist. I knew I didn't actually believe that they were, I just had not known what to expect of this place when I had visited before. After all, I did not want to come here then; and it was my mom pushing me toward Boone that had brought me to Appalachian State.

The students started rolling in at the end of the summer, and I couldn't believe how friendly everyone was. On the streets back home, you had to be careful who you were friendly to, and at all times you had to project toughness, just as a matter of protecting yourself. But the kids I began to meet now were great: open, welcoming, and very different from any idea I might have had about "kids from the 'burbs."

I guess I had presumed they would be preppy and maybe stuck-up at the very least. As it turned out, those App State kids were more about experiencing the outdoor life. This school attracted folks who liked being around mountains and woods. Pretty quickly they exposed me to activities like rafting, tubing, canoeing, and hiking. Needless to say, this was a whole different world for me.

There was one little spot only App State kids knew about, where there was a beautiful waterfall that almost seemed to break through the trees. There was a big boulder nearby where you could stretch out with friends and do homework. There I was, soaking it all in and thinking, "The 'great outdoors' is pretty great! This world is a long, long way from the sidewalks of West Chicago." I was glad my mom put her foot down and insisted I come here.

I would call my old friends back home and try to explain it all to them, and they could hardly believe it. They would laugh, "You were doing what?" I would say, "Yes, I was horseback riding."

Over the summer, the campus was like a ghost town. But the town was an entirely different place when it filled up with students. The first day they were back, someone put together a big ice cream social. Football players were allowed to go, and I was walking between the social and the weight room when a car suddenly backfired from somewhere behind me—POW! I hit the pavement like a well-trained Marine.

CLARENCE SUTTON

Nobody else even flinched, but where I came from, when you heard a sound like that, you got *down*. You tried to be invisible, if not gone. I was so embarrassed. My buddy was looking down at me, saying, "You okay, man?" I jumped up and said, "I'm so sorry, I'm sorry!"

I was afraid he would figure out I was accustomed to reacting to real gunfire. I didn't want people knowing too much about my background. I was sensitive about that at the time. I had no idea whether I could really fit into this place or not. I only knew I wasn't going to ruin my chance.

The football team made me feel welcome too. I have never had trouble making friends, and that helped. Sometimes, when players move across the country to play football, they struggle to make that transition. Maybe they've been in one kind of place all their lives, a small town somewhere or on the streets, like me. It can be culture shock to leave home and go away to school for anybody, but it can be especially difficult for some. I thrived on it, though. "I don't need to go back to Chicago," I was thinking. "I'll take this."

Opening Up

I held my own in the classroom for the most part. The tutors helped me get caught up and into the right courses. I had earned my Associates Degree from Triton, and most of my credits transferred. I started off with the basic core classes in English, Biology, math, and so on—but before long I was able to sign up for courses in criminal justice, and that's where I had my best learning experiences. App State's instructors were so much better at teaching than any others I had known. They were more interactive, and kept me interested in the material.

One of the professors had come to ASU from Berkeley, in California. He would walk us through crime scenarios, sometimes actually dressing up in costumes to represent different types of people. He would show us how a gun could be hidden, and how a criminal might make his move.

I also enjoyed the diversity of my classmates whom I found fascinating. Even still, none of them came from a background quite like mine. In our classes as I participated in the activities, I would demonstrate how things might really happen on the streets. The professors liked having somebody around who knew something about gang behavior, so I became a big part of those discussions.

I found myself opening up about the Austin community and the various incidents I had seen. I described the time I saw gang members beat and kill a man in front of me. My classmates stared at me in wide eyed astonishment. "Are you kidding me? You saw that? They did what?"

Some of my criminal justice classmates went on to work in law enforcement, for the FBI, or the CIA. I have been impressed by the careers and success many of them have experienced.

I could only smile as I recalled the lingering words that substitute teacher had said to me when I was a kid, to go sit down—that I would never achieve any of my dreams of working in law enforcement.

Sidelined

I found it odd that I had come to App State on a football scholarship, yet in some ways that was the one part of my first year that was disappointing to me. I fit in great with the student body, and I adapted well in the classroom. In my criminal justice classes, I was able to carry an A or B-plus average. I was holding my own.

I didn't play much football that first year. One day at practice, Ron G, a buddy of mine, fell on my knee during scrimmage. I had only played in two games, and just when I had found my stride, I was out of the competition, just like that. I was out for the year.

Some people don't understand what it means to have a sport at the center of your life, only to have it suddenly taken away from you. It's not just a game when it is what got you to college. Even just for a season, it's devastating and it is difficult to feel like you are still part of the team. Again, I let my disappointment and frustration get to me, and I found my momentum slowing. I was down on myself, blaming myself for the injury. You might ask why someone would blame himself for something he couldn't help, but sometimes it just helps to blame someone.

My grades began to slip just as my attitude did. The coaches stay on top of how their players are doing with coursework, so I got called into the coach's office and raked over the coals. Coach McNeill was very direct with me. "Man, what are you thinking about? Think of where you came from, and what it means to be here with a full ride and a chance to move up to the next level. Are you going to throw all that away, because of one setback?" The coaches said what they needed to say in a much more colorful way, and they challenged me without holding back.

I received a medical redshirt, which means that the lost year would not count against my eligibility—three years in my case, to go with my time in junior college. I should have felt fortunate since I would get that lost year back, when I was healthy. But like most kids that age, I was all about the *right now*—I didn't care about my eligibility in 1995—I wanted the 1993 season.

"I've let my team down," I told Coach. "I came here to play, not to hobble around on crutches."

"Get out of your pity party, Sutton. You're just feeling sorry for yourself—take charge of your own life. Keep on top of your grades, do your rehab work on the knee, and watch your attitude. It's time to grow up."

I knew all that was true, and I needed to step up— again. My question was, why did I always have to keep fighting out of something? Why was I the one who had to go the extra distance? I looked around and couldn't see any other kids having to face one challenge after another like I seemed to be doing over and over again.

"Why couldn't I just be a normal kid?" I asked Coach McNeill.

"Because you don't have normal opportunities—you have a chance to do things those other kids can only dream about. You think anything's going to come to you easy? You have to fight for every inch of every victory in your life. Talk about disappointing your teammates! What about your buddies back home who don't get to be here—they're your teammates. Your family who do without you, they're your teammates. What about letting *them* down? That's a choice you make. If you let self-pity beat you, it won't be anybody's fault but yours. You can't go dragging back home, hanging your head because of a knee injury. *Stop whining and start making things happen.* You hearing me, Sutton?"

I remember walking out of that meeting with tears in my eyes, shaken up, angry - but motivated. These coaches were more than coaches—they were cheerleaders for my personal life and my mindset. They knew how to get me moving.

Even then, I remember thinking, "What if every kid in the inner city had people like Coach Kent or Coach Edwards or Coach McNeill on his tail? What if I could learn how to "hype" people like that?" It was in the back of my mind to make use of what I was being taught about taking life on your own terms. I was starting to understand what focus and persistence were about – it meant determination to go after a goal without being sidelined by the first bump in the road— or the second, or the third. But, I was losing count of the bumps I had been over.

5 Back in the Game

As that first year went on, I tackled my grades with fresh energy. I also paid my dues in the weight room and in rehab.

You can come back from a knee injury—kids do it every season—but there's a high price to pay in daily discipline. You can look at it a couple of ways.

One is to give up. There's that one moment when the injury happens, when you plant your foot and your knee is twisted in a direction it wasn't intended to go—maybe when somebody, even your own teammate, collides with you. One little moment, and you're not only done for the season, but you are going to have to put in hundreds of hours of extra work just to get your body back to where it was, just because of that one bad incident. That's not to mention catching up with the guys who have gotten ahead of you while you were out. Sure, it's unfair. Everybody else on the team is playing, celebrating, and they haven't had to go through what you did. Look at it that way and you might become resentful, or you quit. Some do.

Or you can look at it another way. Here's your chance to be stronger than ever. These days the doctors can rebuild your body, as well as a blown-out knee. They can make you so you are good to go. But only you can rebuild the spirit inside you—that requires daily discipline, too.

You have to stay on yourself to think positive thoughts, believe your future is going to shine, and believe you can pull something good out of something bad. You have to do this on the inside or you'll never be able to do the rehab work on the outside. But when you do, when you fight through it, you're going to be a stronger player than you were, because you're going to be a better person. I've seen this happen with a lot of my playing buddies, and I believe it happened to me too. I did the work, I fixed my attitude, and my chance finally came during my second season at Appalachian State, in 1994.

I had actually picked a pretty good season to miss that first year. The '93 season was a transition year for Coach Moore and the Mountaineers. We had gone 4-7. This wasn't the kind of program where a losing record was acceptable, so people were down on App State football—including some of the players. It had been only a couple of years earlier that we had gone to the 1-AA national playoffs. But in my first season, the Mountaineers were a losing team.

I was part of one of those recruiting classes that the coaches count on to turn things around. We had several players who were next-level material, and we knew we could be the class not only to reverse course but to win a championship for App State. We were tight-knit, listening to each other's music in the locker room—everything from hip-hop to country, gospel to rock. Coach Kent and his mixed tapes were right in the middle of it all, and he had us singing his songs. We were determined to be the new leaders, to turn this team around.

One day I was in a meeting as practices were getting started. As one of the position coaches left the room, he looked over at me and said, "You're not worth your scholarship."

I had been working for months to reestablish my place on the team. I had done the physical part and kept my attitude straight. Practice was starting and now this guy was questioning whether I belonged there?

Instead of finding a friend to vent to, the way I handled it was to leave the meeting and head for the weight room. I would blow off steam by taking it out on my muscles. But just as I got started on the first cycle, Coach Kent spotted me and came running. I was too tense to talk or to joke around with this character. I was still fuming.

"Hey, man, they don't think you can handle it," he said. He knew what was up, it appeared the coaches had been talking.

"They don't think you can pick it up," he said. "But I say you have a chance to make it to the next level."

Next level? Play on Sundays? I wasn't even playing on Saturdays yet. I thought I was hearing a bunch of hype. But Coach Kent went on about me making a statement, proving a point. I was being challenged again, and it was up to me to step it up and prove that position coach wrong.

Being challenged as a man is powerful motivation. Coaches understand how it can bring out the best in their players. When coaches talk to an athlete, they will question his manhood and get in his face; that player either rises to the challenge or he backs down. If that happens, they were right—he's not worth his scholarship.

I know Coach Kent believed in me. He had been through that first summer with me, and he knew my feelings ran pretty deep. I had the drive and just needed that fire lit under me again.

Two-a-day practices gave me the opportunity to strap on the pads and hit. That's when a player has the chance to establish his credibility. For example, a quarterback might be able to make a great throw, but can he make it when he knows he's going to be popped a fraction of a second after the ball leaves his hand? A safety like me can have speed, but can he lock up and make a tackle? Can he lay the wood and make the ball carrier feel it the next day? Lots of guys look good in helmets and jerseys, but when you put on the pads, when the hitting starts, that's when you find out if you have a ballplayer.

On my first play, the offense called a pass route to the tight end—that's a receiver built like an offensive linemen, not a skinny flanker, and this guy was an all-conference type. I de-cleated him. I hit him so hard, you could hear the clash all across the field; a blow like that makes everybody stop and turn their heads.

I had been doing more than just working out and doing rehabilitation all summer. I'd been in the film room, too. Back at Triton, I had figured out what a difference it could make when you scouted everything in advance. I was on top of the quarterback's cadence, and I knew the instant the snap would come. I had a big head start, recognized the tight end's route across the middle, and I hit him at full speed. I laid my whole body into the hit.

It may have been that one play in practice that earned me the nickname of "Semi" from the team, meaning a semi-tractor trailer or the kind of truck whose path you want to avoid.

The next play was a toss sweep, where the quarterback flips the ball to the running back, who glides around the perimeter with blockers in front of him. Again, I had studied how we ran this play on film, and I was on top of it. With it I brought the pain again. Everybody on the sideline was watching now, screaming and pumping fists. The coach, the one who had made the remark about my scholarship, walked up to me, shaking his head and smiling. "Well done," he said. "That's what we want—right there."

Coach Mac and Coach Kent came running onto the field, a little more enthusiastically. "There ya go! That's what it takes, Sutton!"

At that moment I felt like I had arrived. I was playing ball with some of the most talented players around. This was definitely a couple of steps up from Austin High. I was tackling Terrell Owens, the wide receiver who was at the University of Tennessee at Chattanooga, and then later in my draft class. T.O. holds a number of NFL records. Marrio Grier, also from UTC, went on to play for the New England

Patriots. We had our own guys who were next level—guys like Dexter Coakley, who played ten seasons as a linebacker for the Dallas Cowboys. Matt Stevens was a fellow defensive back, who earned a Super Bowl ring while playing for the Patriots. I knew now that I could run with guys of that caliber.

I had earned my starting job, and the coaches began using me on safety blitz several times during games, knowing I was at my best with a full head of steam and ready to disrupt a play. We did turn the program around, finishing 9-4, five more wins than the previous season. The highlight was beating Marshall, an excellent contender. The previous year, they had beat us 35-3, but in 1994, we played them in Boone during a downpour. They were a 12-2 team that season under Coach Jim Donnan, and two years earlier, they had been national champions. Now, in the rain, we gave them their only loss of the regular season.

I can remember our fans sloshing onto the field to pull down the goalposts, then rocking our bus back and forth. All this excitement seemed crazy considering I had lived through a medical redshirt, a bout with depression, and a 4-7 record. Suddenly everyone on the team was a campus hero. We would go into town and people would ask for our autographs; they wanted to buy us a burger, or have their picture taken with us. Even in class, the professors were giving us the VIP treatment.

When you win, people want to know who you are; they want some of what you've got to rub off on them. I have found this to be true not only in sports but also in business or anything else. The year before I had been worried about keeping my head up. Now I was worried about it being inflated. Don't get me wrong, I was loving every minute of it.

Life in Boone was fine by me, and my only real concern was that it might not last. I had three years to enjoy being a student-athlete, then I would have to reinvent myself and I had no idea what that would entail. Regardless of what came afterward, I doubted I would ever have as much fun as I was having at that time at App State. It is hard to believe that during that first summer, I had considered ditching it all and going back to Chicago. Now you couldn't pry me away, and Chicago was the last place I wanted to be.

Can't Go Home Again

I avoided going to Austin during the spring breaks, summers and at Christmas vacations. I would visit my family for a couple of days, then I would be ready to move on, usually staying with one of my friends and his family. My mother had no problem with that strategy—she was pushing me back out the door soon after I would come in, not because she didn't love me, but because she loved me *that much*. She knew that if something bad was going to happen to me, it would be in Austin, not in Boone.

I remember going home that first year of college and walking to the convenience store to get Helon a Sunday paper. I walked down the block and saw everything with new eyes—the liquor stores that seemed to pop up on nearly every block, the alcoholics and drug pushers sitting on the curb or hanging out on the corner. I wasn't judging them. They didn't have jobs, they had few options, if any, and I could see how hopeless life was for them. I kept thinking, "Man, I can't be around this anymore, or I'll get pulled into that myself."

Later on, my buddy Rashad and I went to a house party in the neighborhood. I didn't really want to go, because I knew nothing good was likely to happen in that environment. But everybody was saying, "C'mon, you gotta go in, just make an appearance. See what's going down." As soon as I walked in the room, I noticed it was full of gangbangers. Somebody stepped on my foot and almost tripped. When he turned to look at me with stone cold eyes, I simply threw up a hand and said, "Look, man, I'm sorry. I really am sorry, man."

He had a gun. That was just a given; I knew it was there. I could just look back at him the wrong way, or give him the wrong attitude, and the situation might escalate. Barely inside, I was already backing off, working through the crowd to get out the other door. All I could think of was what I had at college, and how I didn't want to lose it.

I've read this headline too many times. A kid goes off to school to play football or basketball, he's doing great, then the next thing you know he's found dead back home, in the old neighborhood, or he's in trouble for something else.

As I write this book, I learn that Illinois Congressman Danny Davises 15-year-old grandson was shot when someone broke into their home in the Englewood community in Chicago. It is still happening, the chaos, disruption and pain.

Every day, every minute I spent in Austin, the odds something bad was going to happen increased. "I can't be here," I said to Rashad, so I grabbed him and pulled him out of there with me. At the first possible opportunity, I caught a ride back to North Carolina, then finished my break with my college buddy Kareem Young in Florida. His home was in the Tampa area, and the first thing he did was take me to the mall. Even that was different. I had been to a mall before, but here you could simply do your shopping without having to watch out for who might suddenly pull out weapon.

Kareem also took me to the beach—so I had been to the mountains, seen breathtaking waterfalls and walked mountainous trails, and now I have been to a Florida beach. The world has some great places to experience once you get away from the streets. I felt no need to go home for long visits after that. Kareem, by the way, has coached strength and conditioning for App State, worked with IBM, and has a community support non-profit agency in Florida, called Lift Health.

As I would visit nice places like Tampa and Clearwater, or Winston-Salem with my friend Michael Holliday, a part of me thought, "This is the life. I don't need Austin." But there was another part of me, deep inside telling me, "Or—you can go back to those streets and make a difference. Those kids don't know what is available beyond their lives on the streets. You have a responsibility to open their eyes. Show them what's possible. Teach them what you've learned."

Maybe this was part of the plan. Perhaps it wasn't all about me, but the people I could help.

Building a Team

In 1994, during my second year at App State, the team was pointing to 1995. That was going to be our year. My class of recruits would be juniors for the most part (senior year for me) and we had the chance to show leadership and build on the turnaround we had experienced in '94. The Mountaineers won four games the year I was injured, the following year we won nine. Now we wanted to show everyone that we could win them all.

One of the keys to bringing about a winning team was for us, the upperclassmen, to mentor the younger kids. If you're going to have a strong football program, the juniors and seniors needed to bring along the freshmen and sophomores. We wanted to leave a legacy for the teammates who came behind us. Remembering how I felt when I first joined the program, and not knowing anybody, I made it a point to work with the incoming class.

I mentored some guys, and it felt really good. I discovered something about myself—I could help somebody younger than me. That meant something to me. Maybe I had what it took to help others. Lorenzo Goganious later said to me, "When I came in, nobody would talk to me. I felt left out. But you took me under your wing when nobody else would. You were humble, even though you were established as a starter. Semi, you made it much easier for me."

Lorenzo was a kid who had come from a background much better than mine. He had a brother who played in three Super Bowls, yet he felt left out. Ironically, someone like me, with all the issues I had brought to the table, could make a difference with him!

Mentoring means building friendships you hope to keep for life. Elando Johnson was a cornerback who came in to play behind Matt Stevens, who had gone on to play All-American. I took Elando under my wing and we are still close today, and we always will be. He's one of the best people I know.

Mentoring was also about much more than just football. We made it a point to hang out with the younger players. We listened to Coach Kent's crazy music with them, and learned the words to the songs together. We were building a family, not just a team.

Next Level

Our first game that season was at Wake Forest, an Atlantic Coast Conference team at the 1-A level. We played in the Southern Conference, at the 1-AA level. A team like Wake Forest had a bigger budget, more scholarships, and players who were used to playing such teams as Clemson or Florida State. So we weren't expected to win the game against the Demon Deacons.

We beat Wake, 24-22, on their ground. They were an hour and a half down the highway, so this was a big deal. The coaches told me I put together a highlight-reel performance in that game, getting through three times on the safety blitz.

Coach Mac called it the "Stabber," and I loved it— fifteen yards at full speed into the Wake backfield.

Coach Mac knew how to push my buttons before a big game. "There's a Scout for the Patriots up in the box today, and he's here to see you," he would say, or "Forty-Niners are talking about you, want to see if you've got a Sunday kind of performance in you." I would just blow it off—I wasn't going to believe NFL scouts were traveling to see me play. Dexter Coakley? Sure, I could believe he was a next-level guy. But I didn't have any puffed up ambitions about myself. As the season wore on, though, and we kept winning, it was getting easier to think big, to dream big. We were all making plays, and we believed we could beat any team on any field. We all felt next-level.

We beat Marshall for the second straight season, on their field. The only other team that beat them in the regular season was N.C. State. Marshall had a freshman quarterback named Chad Pennington who would go on to play a lot of seasons in the NFL. I was seeing—and beating—guys with that kind of talent every week. I was also beginning to think I was somebody, too.

We won our conference and got championship rings. Appalachian was a school of proud tradition, and this too was something to celebrate. We were the first North Carolina team in Division I to go undefeated. My college career couldn't have finished on a stronger note, and I realized something—if I hadn't had that medical redshirt two years ago, I would have missed this. I would have played out that first year when I wasn't nearly as good, and finished up by last season. I was beginning to see that sometimes things do happen for a reason.

The big question now was—what happens next? As much fun as I was having, I knew the clock was ticking. The difference between Boone and heaven is that Boone doesn't last forever. A scholarship runs out. You get your degree and it's time for the next chapter.

I had never experienced anything close to a normal life, much less the comfort, peacefulness and possibilities I now knew. I was fearful that when App State was finished with me, the bubble would burst and I would fall back into the old life and all its limitations. I couldn't stand the thought of going back to the auto shop and fixing carburetors and patching tires for the rest of my life. Maybe I could get a job at the Kroger in Boone, sacking groceries or something, I would be fine with that.

I knew for sure that wasn't going back to the streets of Austin – not unless they dragged me, kicking and screaming, and that would not be an easy feat.

Anticipation

For young football players from Pop Warner leagues on up, playing national football on a Sunday is the ultimate dream. But the odds of an athlete making it that far are enormous. Consider this, there are 32 NFL teams with about 250 spots to fill each year. There are approximately 73,000 athletes competing for those open spots, 16,000 will be eligible and eventually only 1.9% of those will be picked. It's a tough road to get to play college football, even harder to play pro. Still, if you do get to play the college game, you can't help but think about the "what ifs." You dream about it, hitting the lottery of athletic life.

As a senior college player, the pros are so close you can almost taste them. All that glory, the chance to play ball at the highest level, national television, commercial endorsements, and sports-affiliated deals landing at your feet. You could be financially set for life if you can just crack the two-deep, get past those safeties and keep running. Most of us come to believe we are good, or we would never have made it as far as college ball.

There is a chance you won't get drafted. If so, then you go for a practice squad, the NFL's version of college scout teams, and even that is an amazing experience. You're being paid decent money to play the game you love without the schoolwork. And, you're rubbing shoulders with the rich and famous. For example, Shannon Sharpe, former Broncos and Ravens player, got into the league as a seventh-round pick. He started on a practice squad, and eventually worked his way up to being an All-Pro, Hall of Fame player. There are lots of stories like that and proof that there is more than one route to the big time.

The locker rooms were all a buzz, Jamie Coleman and Matt Stevens were going to be drafted. Chattanooga had some talent, so did Marshall and other teams we played. We all knew guys who were going to have a shot at the NFL, but now we were hearing from players' agents who wanted to represent us. I just couldn't believe I was one of those guys. It was too good to be true, too good to get my hopes up.

I was looking at more realistic possibilities, and that's why I didn't put my future on hold, waiting on the Big Dream, as some guys do. Using my criminal justice studies, I had begun serving an internship with an attorney in Boone. I knew there would always be job opportunities in some form of police work or investigations. Barring that, I wasn't going to be too exacting. If it came down to it, I would take any honest line of work to keep me off those Austin streets.

Then one day, a buddy of mine got a letter from the NFL— the golden ticket, an invitation to the Indianapolis Scouting Combine. This was the big, annual talent pool for all college players ready to enter the NFL draft. Each team was represented. The coaches, general managers, and scouts looked at the best two hundred players in college football as they performed physical and mental tests, and this would be their shot at the NFL. It was all becoming real.

The trials were physically strenuous and mentally challenging as you ran, you hit, you leaped, you took tests of various kinds—intelligence tests, blood tests, you name it, everything about you was measured and evaluated.

If you could get into the Combine, you would have a shot to play on Sundays. If you showed out at the Combine, if you had your fastest day, used your best ball skills, top vertical leap, and all your other skills were on target, you could move upward in the draft projections—and that could mean the difference in millions of dollars. In other words, you could walk out of there with a shot at a big contract and a signing bonus, or at the least, a chance to catch on with a squad.

My buddy got his invitation, then another friend received his. As you can imagine, I was watching the mail. For me though, nothing but junk. Pretty quickly I assumed I wasn't on the invitation list. I was excited for my friends, but honestly, I was disappointed for myself. Just when I felt I was on top of my game, getting passed up for the Combine meant the end of football for me. Soon I would be finished with classes, so it was time to get real, give up dreaming, and figure out what my next move in life would be. To clear my head, I decided to get in a good workout, so I went to the weight room.

As I started my routine, I heard a familiar voice shouting my nickname, "Semi! Semi!" It was Coach Kent, and he was really worked up about something. "You come here, Big Boy!" He was out of his mind about something, which for him, wasn't unusual. But the man was galloping toward me, so I braced myself, and he tackled me the way I tackled receivers. He hit me so hard, my wrist hit the wall, my Mickey Mouse watch shattered, and I was lying on the floor groaning.

Coach Kent was on top of me, grinning down at me, with a cheek full of tobacco that I could smell. He yelled, "I'm so proud of you, Semi! I'm so proud!"

I tried to fill my lungs again, and said, "What are you talking about?"

His face disappeared behind a piece of paper that he pushed into my face. "Read it! Read it, Big Boy!"

I pushed the coach off me, pulled myself up and looked over the letter. I saw the red, white, and blue NFL logo that is recognized all around the world. So what? This must some kind of flyer or advertisement, and Coach Kent probably got the wrong idea about it, I thought.

"Don't you see what it is?"

Finally I saw my name, the word *Combine*, and the words, "You are cordially invited . . ." The truth finally sank in – I was going to Indianapolis!

Coach Kent was laughing, punching my shoulder over and over, and chattering. He could remember when I was a lonely kid living in the ref's quarters who talked to nobody. He remembered where I had started, and how far I had come.

I was just trying to read the page and take it in. I felt faint. How was this even possible? The word was, if you got the invitation, you were "The Man," one of two hundred in the entire galaxy. You now had a shot with an NFL team—it was just a matter of whether you got drafted or went free agent.

Mountaineer teammates Keyshawn Johnson and Matt Stephens were going. Terrell Owens would be there, and so would Ray Lewis. I recently read an article about that '96 Combine, and how it led to one of the most talented NFL drafts ever, particularly for wide receivers—the guys I had to line up against.

Indianapolis

Walking around that field, seeing the faces of coaches and media people I knew from television was a surreal experience for me. I recognized the famous helmet-hair of

Jimmy Johnson, who was headed to Miami to coach the Dolphins.

Tony Dungy, coach of the Tampa Bay Buccaneers, sat down to talk with me, and afterwards he said, "I can tell you're a deep guy." He couldn't have been nicer and gave me his personal cell phone number. Later, we would have more conversations about topics other than football.

I even ran into a guy I knew from the neighborhood— just a kid I had grown up with. I asked him, "What are you doing here?"

He looked back at me and said, "What are *you* doing here?"

"I'm trying out for the NFL."

"What? You? Clarence Sutton—no way, man! You're just messing with me, right?"

He and I had not seen or heard from one another since I left Austin, and it was hard to believe we were standing there together then. He walked away shaking his head. Most people from Austin would have done the same. I might have been dead or in prison for all they knew, but I was here on the field with the best players of my generation.

During the trials, I felt I performed pretty well, particularly in the shuttle, where I had one of the highest scores, just behind Texas A&M's Ray Mickens. Then it was over and there was nothing to do but wait. Of course I really wanted to be drafted because that would mean a good contract and financial security. But taking the free agent route would not bother me either. I liked the idea of having options.

When it was time for the draft in April, I was ready to hear about my future. The rounds went on, first, second, third, fourth, etc. My name wasn't called—not that I had expected to go high, or even go at all, but I remained hopeful. Then the phone rang right before the seventh and final round. It was the Chicago Bears—my hometown team. At the Combine, I had not seen any indication that the Bears were interested in me at all.

"We're looking at taking a running back, Michael Hicks out of South Carolina State, or we may grab you with that last pick," the guy said. "Then we'll make you a free agent offer. Just be ready, because we're going to call right back either way."

"Yes sir."

I saw Hicks' name go up—he was the final selection for Chicago—and then, sure enough, the phone rang. "How would you like to be a Chicago Bear, Clarence?"

"Yes sir." Which was my way of saying, *abso-freakin-lutely!*

6 Chicago

My plan was to fly to Chicago the very next day. What I thought about as the plane came off the ground was that I had come to Boone by bus, on my own dime, a nobody. Here I was now, leaving on a big bird, on the NFL's dime, toward the next level. No more battered red duffle bag, no more living in closets.

As I came off the plane, I saw a man holding a sign with my name on it—and people were cheering. I couldn't believe it. Cheering for a free agent? People from my neighborhood had come out to welcome me. To them, I was returning a hero, giving autographs to little kids and being escorted to a town car—I had never been in a town car before.

Still dizzy from all the fanfare, a thought continued running through my mind: How can I use all this? How can I take it back to the streets and help people on the west side?

Shortly after arriving in Chicago, I found myself on a tour of the Bears' facility. The weight rooms, the locker rooms, and everything else was first class. Somebody was educating the new players about the city, telling us to avoid certain neighborhoods, and naming places that I had more than a passing familiarity.

I was thinking: *Not on your life. I'm not avoiding any of that. I'm going back to the 'hood, but I'm going back on my own terms.*

My life had changed forever, and I had to believe it was for a reason. It was all too unlikely unless there was a purpose. And I would soon discover what that purpose was.

The Pros

One of the first things they told us at the Bears complex was to stay away from certain parts of town. In other words—the "bad parts." I couldn't help but chuckle at that. They held up a map of Chicago for all the rookies and free agents to see. I had lived most of my life in those areas they were telling us to avoid, and I wasn't going to steer clear of the place where my parents lived, or where my lifelong friends were. I planned on visiting my mother regularly. Plus, I wanted to talk to some of the kids in the area, and show them an example of someone who did not give up, and did not give in to the hopelessness of poverty and crime.

Some guys make it out of there and never look back. I can understand why they feel that way. While I was away at App State, still earning my degree and trying to figure out what to do with my life, that was a time to stay away and keep my nose clean. But now, the way I saw it—this was the time to start trying to make a difference.

I gathered some of the players on the team and said, "Come on, I'm going to show you the 'hood."

It was kind of funny to hear these world-class athletes in their deep voices, say, "We can't go there!"

"You guys are big and strong. You can handle it. Let's go," I said.

I showed the guys the sights of Austin and where to get the best food. Our shiny, new cars caused quite a bit of commotion when we drove up. I had not considered that aspect of our visit when we got out and started throwing the ball around. With no media around, no TV cameras, or anything having to do with public relations, we played a simple game of football with some of the kids in the neighborhood. Word got out and people started showing up from around the block. They were stunned and couldn't believe some of the Chicago Bears were dropping in to throw the ball with them.

We created a sensation in Austin that day, but that wasn't my intention. I just wanted to show some of the guys where I grew up. Now I wondered, "Have I messed up? Is this why they told us not to come here?"

But I saw the excitement in the faces of those Austin kids. They knew about all of us—not just the starters on the team, but rookies and free agents too—everybody. I had a lot of fun that day. Football was great, but something about this experience felt really special. We went back to see our new friends three or four times, and I started to realize there was something there, something that felt really good and meant more to me than a game. My true passion was in connecting with those kids.

The Bears' headquarters were in Lake Forest, on the North Shore. It was an affluent neighborhood, the direct opposite of the Austin community. To get to Lake Forest, you had to go through Austin. I knew the roads pretty well, and I would zigzag through the neighborhoods and the side streets, trying not to be late for team meetings.

One day I was driving back to Lake Forest after a visit with my mom. I was cutting it really close to the time I needed to be back, so I stepped on the gas. Almost immediately, I saw the blue light and was pulled over by a police car. The officer took a look through the window, saw this young man with dark skin driving a nice little sports car, and I felt I could almost read his mind. He was slightly rude when he looked at my license, and I was thinking that I really couldn't afford to be late for a team meeting. As a free agent, I didn't need anything that made a bad impression.

I said, "I hope this won't take too long. I can't be late for my team meeting."

"A meeting for what kind of team?" asked the officer.

"Football team. Chicago Bears," I replied.

He just looked at me, looked back at my license, then returned to his cruiser. After saying something on his radio, it wasn't long after that a swarm of black-and-whites came screeching up with their sirens blaring. I wondered what I had done or said—and hoped I was not going to be locked up.

One officer walked up to my window and asked, "So how many games we gonna win?" Another officer handed me a piece of paper and a pen. He wanted my autograph. A few others did the same and all of them wanted to talk football.

The rudeness was gone. I delighted in their enjoyment of the occasion, and it was all good, except by this time I was really going to be late for my meeting. I excused myself and thundered away. They didn't even flinch at my exiting speed.

To people like that, someone being in the NFL changes everything. You become a VIP. To my mom, though, I was the same son, the same kid I had always been. She was proud I was playing NFL ball, but not as proud as she was that I had earned my degree in criminal justice. I had a college education and I had stayed out of trouble. That's what counted most. For her, life was good. Helon would occasionally come to the practices, and he seemed proud and happy as well.

Sometimes when I returned to Austin, I would visit the old auto shop and pick up a broom, or help out with odd jobs. It didn't occur to me to worry about getting some new, expensive suit and tie greasy because I did not wear expensive suits and ties; I did not go for any of that. Some of the players wore clothing that cost thousands of dollars, and they couldn't believe I was still wearing the same stuff.

"Why are you wearing a pink suit?" I once asked a teammate.

"Hey, this suit cost three thousand, man! Respect this suit."

"It's a pink suit, man. Pink!" They would shake their heads at me. I shook mine back at them.

The people from my neighborhood were also surprised that I would be hanging around an auto shop, changing a flat tire, instead of cruising in my 300ZX, or picking out a night club to hang in that evening. My agent had gotten me that car, but I wasn't going to throw my money around. I knew even then I wouldn't be in the league forever, and I was going to save while I could.

Interception

Fans may not care much about preseason games; established starters may not care about them either. But for rookies and free agents, those games in August meant everything. Once the season starts, you may not get a chance to show what you can do. But in the NFL, the second half of an exhibition game is your time. Generally, the starters and the two-deep rotations play in the first half. After halftime, the coaches bring in the rookies and free agents, people who aren't in the current plans for the season.

I did get to play a good bit in three games, and I was pushing for time particularly because it would mean something to the kids back on the streets. Of course, they were mostly interested in meeting the better known players and they would always ask me to come back and bring some of them with me. I knew they were watching us on TV, and I wanted to shine for them. I think it also gave me a little street credibility.

We had a game with the Miami Dolphins, and I was excited because Dan Marino, who was about to retire, was a name that meant something to me. See, I saw most players as "college all-stars," good players but not intimidating—I could compete with them; they just had a little head start on me. But a guy like Marino was a legend.

We played the Dolphins at home, and I was fired up to play for my friends and family against Marino. But one of the coaches wasn't straight with me on his plans to play me. I got frustrated with him and ended up getting into some trouble. It was just a moment of acting out, letting my disappointment get the better of me. As a result, I was asked to go apologize to the coaches. I had been playing some special teams and was beginning to do well, but this set me back. They let me know I had to prove I belonged there, even more than before. When you are trying to make it as a free agent, there is very little margin for error.

I did play in the second half of the Miami game and did well. The following Saturday, I played in New Orleans at the Dome. But my time on the field wasn't enough to keep my place. Two days later, I was on the waiver list with a number of other players. I had been cut from the team.

Looking back, I don't know whether I could have stayed on the roster for a full season, but one mistake was too much to overcome. I was crushed, of course, because I knew I was good enough. I knew I could put in the work and play at the highest level of football.

Later that night, I was on the phone with my agent, asking about our next move. He said there was some interest from the Kansas City Chiefs and even the Montreal Alouettes, a Canadian Football League team. After considering our options, my wife and I decided to travel to Beaumont, Texas, where they had right kind of facilities for training and preparing to try out for the Chiefs.

Shannon

Shannon and I met Boone and became good friends, and she later became my wife. She started her college career at East Carolina as a track athlete, but when she tore her Achilles tendon she ultimately transferred to Appalachian State. Her father worked in a church ministry, and her family had carried out mission work all over the world.

Because of her background and how grounded she was in her faith, Shannon helped me understand new insights about helping people. She knew what missions were, and she was the first to recognize that I had a passion for helping that went even deeper than playing football. She always encouraged that passion.

"This is what you're here for," she would say. "This is what really gets you excited, connecting with kids who need encouragement and guidance."

While we were at App State, Shannon didn't know I played football. When you're an athlete, it seems that people focus only on that. I was used to the fact that some people were around me just because of what I could do on the football field, so I gravitated toward Shannon, who seemed to care about me because of who I was as a human being. Shannon shared her perspectives, and she helped me keep it real from the time I was in Boone through the time I was back in Chicago.

When we arrived in Beaumont, and settled into our living quarters, I began training. It was going well, but there was something strange going on, my feet were burning, and I couldn't figure out why. My hamstring also burned, and I could feel it all the way down to my heels. I went to a doctor to get a full checkup.

"You have nerve damage," the doctor said.

"What? How could I have nerve damage? I haven't done anything to my feet or to my legs—just the normal bumps and bruises. Football stuff, right?"

"Think about how you tackle," said the doctor. "Do you ever lead with your head?"

"Yeah, I guess I do. If you play hard and fast in football, you fly into people and your helmet might get there first. Particularly at the safety position."

"Well, let me tell you something, Clarence. If you keep playing ball, you'll be in a wheelchair by the time you're forty."

I was stunned and didn't know how to respond to what I was hearing. A wheelchair?

Today, as I write this, we have all become more aware of, and have learned a lot about head trauma, and the long term physical effects while playing football. A lot of guys paid a hefty price for years of physical poundings taken on the field in the NFL. But at the time I was playing, there wasn't a lot of concern about that. As a safety, I was going to be hitting people in the open field. You either gave it one hundred percent, or you found some other line of work. It was one hundred percent or not at all.

I went back to our place and talked to Shannon about it. She already knew where my future lay, but I wasn't so sure.

If it didn't work out with Kansas City, my intentions were to fly up to Montreal, get a physical there, and give football one more shot. I actually had my airline ticket in hand. But Shannon gently reminded me, "You have a larger calling. You can find a place to help kids wherever we go." Because of her faith, she understood about being called to help others.

"I've just been volunteering," I said. "How am I supposed to support a family like that?" We had not been married long, but we knew we wanted to have children, and I wanted to be able to provide for them.

"You can build your own company," she said. "You can make a career out of it. I know you have it in you."

I wasn't sure if I had a lasting career in football any longer. I'd have to make the roster again every new season. It was a young man's game, and I had a doctor who was insisting I was headed for a wheelchair if I kept playing

On the other hand, helping people was something that gave me joy. I saw football as a means to get that done. I had always planned to use my NFL connections for opportunities to make a difference to help those in need. And difference-making was something you could do until the day you died; unlike football, which might get you through your twenties and maybe a little into your thirties. I thought about it and realized it wasn't such a tough decision after all. "I'm done," I told Shannon. "Done with football."

Shannon understood, but a lot of our friends and family didn't. When word got out that I was walking away from football, some were pretty upset. I received calls from people trying to get me to turn around and from those asking why would I give up on something I had worked so hard to achieve, something millions of people only dreamed about. I was living the dream, in their opinion. I was a few good practices, a few quick seasons away from becoming a starter, then a millionaire. And I wanted to do what? Social work? Talk to street thugs and gangbangers?

A lot of my buddies from past teams told me I was making a mistake. My agent said, "Are you kidding? Why do you need to do this? You don't have to choose between these lives. You're already doing good things. You've got off-season to do that stuff. You'll never get this chance to play on Sundays again, if you walk away. Never."

"It's a wrap," I told him. Don't get me wrong, I continued to think about it, wondering if I was doing the right thing, but I kept coming to the same conclusion about who I was and what I wanted.

Sometimes you realize the real dream in your heart isn't what you thought it was. The kid who sat on the bike in Oak Park, looking at the mansions through the rail fences, and said, "It's got to be possible to break through to a better life," still existed deep inside me.

Along the way, through all the ups and downs, I did learn something. I realized that the "better life" wasn't all about money. For me, it was about becoming someone who made the world a better place— someone who taught others how to have hope.

During the previous months I had already been volunteering and providing some counseling while I was in

Chicago. Then, when I went to Beaumont I helped counsel kids involved in the Texas Juvenile Probation program. The work I was doing was only supposed to be a temporary thing, but I continued to work with kids who had gotten into trouble and were awaiting trial. During that time, that work became a paying job.

We were in Beaumont for a little while, and our first son, Corey, was born. Beaumont was a good place for us, we focused on our future, our baby boy, and began routing a new, unknown path.

Where would this path lead us? When I was a kid in college, I enjoyed living in North Carolina. I had also visited Charlotte as a Bear when we played against the Carolina Panthers. I knew it was a growing city. Shannon and I liked Charlotte and we also liked Portland, two very different places. We decided that every big game begins with a coin toss, so we literally tossed a coin.

Afterward, we packed up our things and drove to North Carolina to begin a brand new life.

7 A Different Life

I decided to start this new life by enrolling in the police academy, still remembering what that substitute teacher had said to me long ago. I had achieved one of my goals in football, and had one more to go to prove him wrong on both counts.

Law enforcement worked well with my degree in criminal justice, and I wanted to understand that side of working with kids. The academy was a good experience—I broke all their physical fitness records without too much effort, and I was actually the valedictorian of my class. I had lots of advantages when I entered the police academy. My understanding of life on the streets, my athletic training, and what I had learned in the classroom at App State all proved to be valuable lessons in this new career.

Above all else, I was also beginning to understand how important it is to have good character. You can have all the training in the world, you can be an Olympic champion, and you will still be a failure if you don't understand and love people. It was as though I was wired to connect with and encourage people of all kinds, and the more troubled they were, the more I accepted the challenge to try and help them.

I enjoyed what I was doing. If you plan to work with people who have mental health issues, you better have some knowledge of what that is all about before you start. You need to recognize that you will encounter situations that are difficult to see, hear and understand. If helping those kinds of people is not a part of who you are, you would be better off doing something else.

I knew I could handle it. Shannon thought of it as my calling, and my new work tended to confirm that I had made the right choice.

One night, while working on the police force, I was asked to assist an older married couple who were "regulars" at the assignment desk. They would do their drinking on weekends, get into loud fights, and someone would eventually call the police. Typically, there was nothing dangerous about this kind of assignment, but most officers would rather be doing something else. The couple's ages were somewhere between sixty-five and seventy years old.

When I showed up, they were surprised. I didn't seem much like a cop to them, but we hit it off. I found it easy to make them laugh, and soon they forgot why they had been fighting in the first place. I was there for several hours, and it turned into a social visit. Yet, I had been instructed to be prepared to deal with them physically. I defused their emotions, got them laughing, and nobody had to be tackled or held down.

The next time that couple got rowdy, I received the call again. Pretty soon they were calling the police station and asking specifically for me. They weren't mad—they just wanted to hang out. And if they needed to, they would stage a fight just to get me dispatched their way.

Because I was a young African American and the couple was southern Caucasian, the other officers seemed surprised at my ability to break through potential barriers. But, I received a ribbon for helping that couple work out their problems. I have always believed that people have the same issues, whoever they are, wherever they live, whatever race or sex they may be. Those things only make a difference if we let them.

Before long, I realized I was actually enjoying myself, I was helping people, and it was clear I wasn't missing football so much after all.

Not every assignment was as easy as that rowdy couple. My first day on the job, we received an emergency call from a private residence. My partner and I went to the house to investigate. When we arrived, a man stepped out and said, "My wife was really upset. I couldn't get her to listen to me." We peered inside and discovered she had just shot herself in the head.

I looked around and noticed a little girl. She immediately became my priority. This scene, the emotions, the fear, the chaos took me back to my own experiences growing up and seeing things no child should see. Not every cop can relate to something like that if he hasn't lived through that kind of incident, but I was thinking, *somebody needs to talk with this girl*.

I took her away from the scene and spoke softly to her, telling her everything was going to be all right. We were able to defuse the situation. Later I was told that most rookies would not have been able to handle seeing that level of gun violence on their first day—a body, all that blood, people panicking. But my life had prepared me well.

Law enforcement suited me, but it was never my end goal. I was there for the experience I knew would be invaluable later, and also to prove to myself that I could do it.

I became a trainer for the State of North Carolina on weekends, traveling here and there to teach people self-defense and other physical requirements of protecting and serving. There weren't too many cops around who had trained for the NFL, and I found that police officers, particularly the men, seemed to be in awe of working with a former football player. For example, we were eating lunch at a Jack in the Box restaurant, when a report of shots fired came over the radio. We jumped in our vehicles and hurried to the scene as fast as we could. When we arrived, another officer was there crouched behind his car door. We saw a guy with dreads, sprinting away from the scene. When I pulled up close to the officer, he yelled, "You stay in the car, and we'll cut him off."

But I had a different plan in mind. Football prepares you for this kind of thing, particularly when you play in the defensive backfield. I leaped out of the car and started to chase the suspect. I had that old adrenalin rush, and I pushed it too hard too quickly—so that my hamstring locked up! I was down on the ground while the other officers were still on foot chasing him. I hobbled back to my feet—and passed the other cops as we all chased the suspect down. I was still that fast, even with a pulled hamstring, and after taking a fall. That was the kind of thing the other cops just shook their heads over.

The other officers enjoyed laughing about my mishap over the next few days while I was limited to desk duty, answering the phones and waiting to heal.

I applied for a job with the state to broaden my knowledge of the mental health field. A huge advantage of working for the state was that the diagnosis training I would need was provided and paid. By understanding how the government functioned, and through making a commitment to learn how to improve the types of programs they provided, I would be making progress toward eventually opening my own practice, which was my ultimate goal. I needed to be in the middle of it so I could understand how it worked and what it offered.

I was extremely fortunate as I made the transition to the mental health profession. I was hired by the state, and trained under really good people who taught me a great deal. When I started, I had no clue what I was doing. I worked with Karen Andrews who was the director of Pathways Mental Health in Gastonia, North Carolina. She oversaw millions of dollars in funding, so among the things she helped me understand was how the budget worked, a major part of navigating the system. People like Karen and Steve Wilhelm, who created the wilderness program for the state, condensed decades of valuable training into just a few years for me. The right people were there for me at just the right time – again.

In addition, the timing couldn't have been more perfect when, just as I was making my transition to the mental health field, the state decided to divest itself from certain public services, pushing them to the private sector. The private sector was where I wanted to be all along. The training and experience I had gained through working with the state was paying off. Now, in 2001, instead of having to go out on my own, and shoulder all the pressures and challenges of starting up a new business, the state decided that was exactly what they wanted—people like me to take on their caseloads. They were willing to do a lot of things to help make that happen. What this meant was that in many cases, I could move clients I was already working with to my new private practice. I didn't have to start from scratch.

Twenty-five people transferred from state employment to our new practice—twenty-five people began serving under me. They had faith in my leadership and in the fact that, while I wasn't high on experience in this field, I was equipped with life experiences and relationship skills.

I hired a therapist, someone trained and accredited to do individualized therapy. I hired my first case manager and a direct care staff, so we had good people to go one-on-one with clients. The state continued to make referrals to us, which helped a lot. While learning on the job myself, I was able to hire two doctors and more than seventy-five one-on-one caseworkers.

The transition went very smoothly. The state government, of course, was pleased we were able to make a solid transition from government to the private sector, and this led to a number of other health providers coming to North Carolina.

It is amazing how things work out. I may not have had a long career in the NFL, but that didn't matter to the kids or their parents I worked with. Because for a while, I had been with the Bears which helped me to build relationships as a probation officer, as a policeman, and later as I moved into mental healthcare.

Touchdown!

At Carolina Therapeutic Services and Chicago Therapeutic Services, our programs focus on children. Our mission is to rescue them, not only physically but mentally and emotionally as well. We want to help them believe in themselves and their potential to make life what it should be.

Too many children lose their hope before they even get started. We work to build relationships with them one-on-one, and challenge them to make things happen in their lives. We work with their families, using all our expertise to help them bond together and become what a family is supposed to be, nurturing and supportive. Family values, we have found, don't always come naturally. We model those values in the family atmosphere of CTS, the way we relate to each other, the way we respond to our clients.

When you walk into one of our facilities, you might think you're in a typical doctor's office. We operate with all those structures in place, but once you deal with us, you're going to find you are in a warmer and more caring environment than most traditional medical centers offer. We go out to the schools to help teachers and students deal with motivational or grade issues. If gangs are an issue, we don't shy away from that, as some would. Even while I was still playing football, I was starting to talk to gang members, because I understood how they think and how I should talk to them. We believe we can go into any community and make it a healthier place for families and kids to build a life.

We also work with children in need of out-of-home placements. Sometime crises occur, and parents are not always available for the child. Maybe one of them left sometime in the past, and the other has been in an accident, suffered an illness, or is homeless. Perhaps the child has been abandoned. We step in to find a caring, temporary home for the child. If there have been problems in the child's home, we make sure those homes learn to function as they should. If reunification is impossible, we find permanency for the children through adoption.

Our success in Gastonia, North Carolina, where we are based, has allowed us to expand throughout the state. It made sense that we would continue to grow our services into new areas with varied needs, places such as Asheville, Lenoir, and further northwest. We eventually began opening offices in South Carolina and Illinois.

I think there were some folks who believed that as a black man, I would be more effective in the inner city—places like Austin—and that I wouldn't get too far in the rural areas of the South. Too many people rely on those types of labels and the differences they perceive between us.

I see it very differently. People are people. They have the same issues, whether they live in a housing project in a major city, a small town, or out in the country. Problems are problems. At the same time, I make sure our staff are culturally competent, and that we have people of all ethnicities and backgrounds involved in our mission. Doing so enables us to work with diverse populations, even if those populations hold to a certain bias. We have had tremendous success in rural areas, and our referrals continued to grow.

Other providers targeted the cities, but we have found rural areas to be underserved. People in these areas also need access to mental health resources. Not only that, but we want to be relevant in broader settings. If you can do only one thing in one setting, you won't be around very long as a practice. Our philosophy is to work with people of all populations, especially those experiencing circumstances that impede their quality of life. Hope can be found anywhere. Family values can be applied everywhere. A child needs the same basics, wherever he or she lives, and so does the family.

My background, growing up on the roughest streets of Chicago, would be considered a curse by some. But I have come to see it as a blessing, because it helps me to understand people who have lost hope, and who can no longer see or secure the resources available to help overcome their obstacles.

Helon taught me life skills, how to follow through, and to do what you say you are going to do; he compelled accountability which gave me the basis for staying on the right track.

Roy showed me the meaning of hard work and how to understand and follow my intuition.

There was my mother, who believed in me and fought for me to get the best education I could. She taught me to avoid being in the wrong place at the wrong time.

My experience on the football field taught me about fighting hard for something you want, and about making sacrifices for a team.

Shannon was there to illustrate what it meant to have a calling. She believed in me, and helped foster what really counted—the desire to help people. In addition, I had a young family, and my focus on caring for them kept me focused throughout building my career.

There were many people in the right place at the right time to help me—a high school coach, a college strength and conditioning director, a professional from Pathways, all who were willing to be patient and teach me what I needed to know. Even the state of North Carolina was there for me. The state said, "Here, we won't be able to allocate people and funds to support these needed programs in the future. Can we hand it off to you?" Though I was not a running back, I was willing to take that handoff.

The common thread that blankets my life is that I am a fighter, I keep moving through the punches, reinventing my approach, and I never give up. I have learn to use whatever setbacks or advantages I encounter to move forward to reach the goals my heart had identified for my future.

I knew I had worked hard, survived the streets, gotten through school and earned a degree. I was privileged to have had the opportunity to play in the National Football League. But the bottom line is that I was fortunate and blessed to have had those experiences, for they shaped me and made me the man I am.

This plan is bigger than me. I believe knowing that is the key to understanding the purpose of your life. Whatever it is you were made to do, whatever that thing is, it is always bigger than you. It will come down to your willingness to recognize and accept the help that is given by the right people when your paths cross. Believe me, they will be there. You just have to realize when it is happening. Then, you will have to decide if you're willing to fight through any obstacles to be the best you can be.

For me, it all started on a bicycle, riding from one side of town to the other, discovering that people lived in all kinds of surroundings. Something deep inside of me kept me from accepting my limitations. I was going to fight. I intended to find out what it was like on the other side of that fence, where people lived in the big houses. And as I have gone through life, sure enough, I have been exposed to people of all kinds.

What else have I learned? It is not about money. It is not about the color of your skin. It is not about hitting the big time and playing NFL football, or being a movie star, or a musician, or some other symbol of fame and power. People are people, and what we all need is hope. What we all need is the belief that we can move forward and participate in our own destiny, to realize we too are capable and worthy of having a happy and meaningful life.

The message I have for children and families is this:

Do not listen to anyone who tells you it can't be done.

Choose your own future and make a plan for it.

Go get it. Take hold of it and hang on.

Adapt to and learn from unexpected challenges.

Be willing to accept those people who may extend a helping hand.

And one other thing—while you're doing that, reach behind you and help someone else do the same.

Carolina Therapeutic Services
Protecting Our Kids With Love

Carolina Therapeutic Services, Inc. is a provider of rehabilitative behavioral health, community support adult services, targeted case management, in-school and out-patient treatment services. We also provide out-of-home placements for children in need of temporary shelter, and adoption services for those children in need of a forever home.

Our *accreditation* through CARF provide the community assurance that we, as an agency, are meeting the clients' needs in quality of care, documentation, health and safety and exceed state and national standards for compliance.

Our *professional teams* are committed to safeguarding the continuity of care through collaboration with all participants involved in the client's treatment process.

Our *organizational structure* is designed to maximize opportunities for persons served to obtain and participate in services provided. Where appropriate, we provide information to the clients in collaboration with stakeholders.

Our *community based services* meet the needs of the

consumers we serve, their natural supports, and the community as a whole. Carolina Therapeutic Services incorporates the philosophical and clinical views of Person Centered Thinking, System of Care, and Trauma Focused CBT, which focuses on instilling hope, identifying, and then increasing the emotional, cognitive, social, and psychological functioning elements of all consumers served.

Clients are served on a *one-to-one* basis according to age, emotional functioning, personality and skill level.

Our *foster care program* includes recruitment, licensing, supervision and monitoring of foster homes for the purpose of receiving children in need of out-of-home placements that are referred to us through child welfare agencies, guardians, schools, or parents. The Care Coordination teams are trained and experienced qualified professionals who support, guide, and work closely with stakeholders and consumers to ensure success in meeting established goals.

Our *guiding principles* include:

- Child/youth and family driven services: We recognize that family is the constant in the consumer's life and that collaboration at all levels of care is important. We believe that keeping persons serviced and their families informed, in an appropriate and supportive manner, is a key to successful treatment.
- Promotion of resilience: Understanding that individuals have many varied experiences and are from diverse backgrounds, we meet the

consumer where they are environmentally, academically, and psychologically in their current circumstance. We assist individuals to increase their ability to properly adapt to stress and adversity. Stress and adversity can come in the shape of family or relationship problems, health problems, or other worries.

- Cultural and linguistic competence: We have training requirements and opportunities in place to increase our staff's ability to gain knowledge and understanding of the diverse populations we serve and offer translation services for those whose first language is not English.

- Strengths-based approach: We recognize strengths and individuality, understand and respect different methods of coping. We emphasize a person's self- determination and strengths and view clients as resourceful and resilient in the face of adversity emphasizing a focus on future outcomes and strengths that people bring to a problem or crisis.

- Trauma-informed care: where applicable, recognizes that people often have many different types of trauma in their lives. People who have been traumatized need support and understanding from those around them. We educate our communities about the impact of trauma. Understanding its impact is an important first step in becoming a compassionate and supportive community.

Locations

Gastonia, NC (Corporate)
Chicago, IL
Columbia, SC
Gaffney, SC
Lenoir, NC
Orangeburg, SC
Rock Hill, SC
SC State University

Donations and Community Development

Carolina Therapeutic Services Community Development is a 501(c)3 non-profit that provides programs to fill some of the needs of the persons in the communities we serve. We offer numerous opportunities for individuals and corporations to participate in various funding efforts, such as the Cassandra Robinson Rising Star Scholarship, Duffles for Dignity, and the Angel Tree Christmas funds.

For more information:

Visit our website at:
http://www.carolinatherapeuticservices.org
Email: info@Carolinatherapeuticservices.com
Facebook.com/CarolinaTherapeuticServices

ABOUT THE AUTHOR

Clarence Sutton was born and raised in the Austin neighborhood of Chicago. A graduate of Appalachian State University in Boone, North Carolina, he studied criminal justice and psychology, and competed in football and track. He signed with the Chicago Bears, though nerve damage abbreviated his NFL career. He is the founder and CEO of Carolina Therapeutic Services, Inc., a mental health provider with offices throughout the south and mid-west.

Made in United States
Orlando, FL
10 May 2022

17712015R00064